The Law, the Prince and the Scribe

Samuel Kutzerfuß

The Law, the Prince and the Scribe

Samuel Rutherford

Catherine Mackenzie

CF4•K

10 9 8 7 6 5 4 3 2 1
Copyright © 2019 Catherine Mackenzie

Paperback ISBN: 978-1-5271-0309-2
epub ISBN: 978-1-5271-0406-8
mobi ISBN: 978-1-5271-0407-5

Published by
Christian Focus Publications, Geanies House, Fearn, Tain,
Ross-shire, IV20 1TW, Scotland, U.K.
www.christianfocus.com
email: info@christianfocus.com

Printed and bound by Nørhaven, Denmark
Cover design by Daniel van Straaten

Scripture quotations are from the Authorised King James Version or the author's own paraphrase.

All rights reserved. No part of this publication may be reproduced, stored in a retrieval system, or transmitted, in any form, by any means, electronic, mechanical, photocopying, recording or otherwise without the prior permission of the publisher or a licence permitting restricted copying. In the U.K. such licences are issued by the Copyright Licensing Agency, Saffron House, 6-10 Kirby Street, London, EC1 8TS. www.cla.co.uk

Author's Note

Throughout this book you will see passages and lines that have been italicised. These are either direct or edited quotes from Samuel Rutherford. He wrote many letters and sermons. I have on occasion slightly edited some of these as the vocabulary Samuel used was often very different to what we use today, and for modern day readers to understand his meaning I felt it was necessary to do this. A minister who writes letters and sermons often gets his inspiration from other times and places. Therefore, I've included some of what Samuel Rutherford wrote in his letters or later sermons earlier on in the story than when they first appeared in print. The incidents in this book are often based on real events, some are based on likely events. Now and again I have used my imagination. For example, conversation and dialogue are sometimes taken from Samuel Rutherford's own words though on occasion these words are imagined in order to get some other point or teaching across. Scripture quotations throughout this book are based on the Authorised King James version as this scripture version is more in keeping with the time period. However, it is more likely that Rutherford would have used another version like the Geneva Bible.

Dedication

To Sam, Carolyn, Joseph and Aletheia Poon.

Thank you for introducing me to my new Scottish hero: Samuel Rutherford.

Thank you Sam for your invaluable help!

CMM

Contents

Samuel Rutherford and You 9

A Wild and Windswept Scribe 15

Songbirds by the Solway 25

Always Writing, Always Preaching.................37

Set Your Arrow Straight.................................47

Letters, a Disguise and Tragedy......................57

Real Friends and Real Enemies......................71

Events Belong to God 81

The King who Huffed and Puffed....................89

Look at Scotland!..................................97

1649 and All That..................................107

Samuel Rutherford's Grave........................115

Samuel Rutherford Timeline......................116

Bibliography..118

Fact File: Anne Cousin....................................119

The Sands of Time are Sinking......................120

Take Away Points...123

Thinking Further Topics................................125

Samuel Rutherford, Democracy and the U.S.A....136

Map...139

Samuel Rutherford and You

The alarm on your phone suddenly wakes you from a deep sleep. You struggle out of bed, bleary eyed about to begin another day of routine – the things that you do every morning without thinking.

Chewing on your cereal, you flick through some news posts sparing little thought for the violence you read of in other countries where men and women fight for freedoms they don't have…. Freedom of speech, freedom to vote, freedom to live. They stand up against injustice and get thrown in prison. They have principles they would vote for – if they were allowed. They long to worship, to read their Bibles without fear of reprisal but even that right, that choice isn't theirs. Now you. You click on a like, share a post, visit a web page and skip over any items that refer to yet another election or referendum. There's a letter stuck to the fridge with a magnet that's from someone who wants to be the next city mayor, but it's covered by vouchers for the supermarket and a bill from the plumber. Then on the calendar there's a memo for a youth Bible study, a

Sunday service, and a prayer meeting. You may or may not choose to go to any of these. That's your life. The life that many Christians in this world of ours would love to have – a life of freedom and choice. This life that you have is a life that people in the past, fought and died for.

Freedom is often something that has been won through sacrifice, but it is also something that could be lost. For now, you are living in a democracy, and have a considerable amount of political and religious liberty. That is something to be thankful for.

But why is it that you have freedom and someone else doesn't? Why this country and not that one? This century and not two hundred or three hundred years ago?

Well, a big part of the answer could be Samuel Rutherford. He is one of the key people behind the liberties that you have such as freedom of worship and freedom of speech. Rutherford had truly remarkable natural talents and a spiritual passion. He loved Christ and God's Word – and this was the power behind everything that he did be it preach a sermon in his church, write a letter to a grieving mother, or publish one of the most important political works of his time. That political work was called *Lex Rex: The Law and the Prince* and was influential in ensuring that men and women in the future would have a say over their lives. *Lex Rex* is the Latin for 'The Law is King'. It's the opposite in fact to the words Rex Lex which mean

Samuel Rutherford

'The King is law'. Samuel disagreed that kings were the ultimate authority. Instead he firmly believed that all people, even kings, should do what God tells them to.

Now the monarchs of Samuel Rutherford's time took exception to that sort of talk. They didn't burn Samuel Rutherford at the stake, but his book *Lex Rex* was set alight in his own land of Scotland. Rutherford described tyrannical kings as men who drank 'the blood of innocents', persecutors intent on destroying the people of the land. These big words brought big trouble on this small-town Scottish pastor. But small-town doesn't mean insignificant. One day Samuel's words and beliefs would stretch far beyond his own little patch of hills and cottages.

Think about one of the most influential democracies of the twentieth century – the United States of America. That nation is famous for its declaration of Independence and its Constitution. Those two documents would not have been written if *Lex Rex* had not been written. America one day became a nation totally independent from any monarchy, but Rutherford wasn't supporting revolution in his book. He also believed that Christians had a duty to obey and respect their rulers as long as those rulers were lawful. If you found yourself in a nation where a tyrant was king – well that was a different matter. If your monarch was persecuting the church, forcing it to conform to unbiblical standards then you were at liberty to take a stand against that monarch. In Samuel's life he experienced what a tyrant and persecution was like. He knew what he was writing about.

You see, the kings of Samuel's lifetime had treated Scotland and her church in a disgraceful way.

Scotland at one point had been a strong Presbyterian nation. The Presbyterian church had been set up in the country by the reformer, John Knox. Presbyterianism was a system of church government that gave the people, under God's Word and an elected church government, the power to make decisions. They could decide who they would have as their preachers and pastors. They could choose how they would worship in their church services. However, in the years before Samuel Rutherford was born, that system of reformed church government had come under attack. King James VI abhorred it, and wanted to force the nation of Scotland to adopt another system altogether. James wanted to gain back control as monarch and head of the church. This system was called Episcopacy. James' son, Charles I, was cut from the same cloth. He even went as far as sending in an army to Scotland when they refused to accept his prayer book and other Roman Catholic practices.

This time of history was certainly dramatic. When you read through the 1600s you seem to go from one conflict to another, from one political upheaval to another. The people of the land were fighting each other, and even a monarch was beheaded. Charles I was executed at the orders of Parliament[1] after he was defeated in the Civil War[2].

This is the backdrop to Samuel Rutherford's life – a world of bloodshed. However, Samuel himself never picked up a sword – unless you describe his pen as a weapon, that he wielded with expertise and flair.

So, if, when reading about the life of Samuel Rutherford, you find his world confusing – you are in good company. His was a world so different to yours and mine we are bound to have questions, some that we just won't be able to answer.

However, what we can do is look at his life, appreciate the beauty of his words, recognise him to be the freedom fighter that he was and be thankful for men like him who stood up for God's Word and the rights of ordinary people.

Maybe your life could be a life like his …

A life that honours God's Law and stands up to princes with love and courage and a pen.

---

1. Parliament: This is a legislative body in the United Kingdom that makes and monitors the laws of the land. In the past it was under the ultimate authority of the monarch until those powers were transferred to the elected Members of Parliament themselves.

2. The English Civil War was a series of battles fought between the Royalists or Cavaliers, and the Parliamentarians, also known as Roundheads. It took place between 1642 and 1651.

A Wild and Windswept Scribe

A lonely figure appeared on the horizon like a dark ink blot. He stood out against the grey storm clouds that were rolling in from the Solway Firth[1]. All he carried with him were a couple of saddle bags containing the tools of his trade: a Bible, books and a pen. Here was a solitary scribe on his way to a new life, new challenges and a new future. There were no people to see him and his mount struggle against the onslaught of the wind and rain – only some sheep and black cattle huddled against trees and gorse bushes. Broad earthen dykes or walls appeared here and there, hinting at the existence of people somewhere, but, on the whole, all the land as far as the traveller could see was wild and windswept and empty. Samuel Rutherford was on the last leg of his journey from Edinburgh to his new home in Anwoth in the region of Galloway in southern Scotland. It was quite a change he realised, as he battled on against the weather. A very different life indeed. Instead of densely

---

1. The Solway Firth is a firth or body of water that forms part of the border between England and Scotland, between Cumbria and Dumfries and Galloway.

populated alleyways with large throngs of people on market days, Samuel was heading towards a country parish with more livestock than humanity. The farms, crofts or clachans as they were sometimes called, were miles apart and there wasn't even, as far as Samuel knew, a village square for people to meet in.

He took some time to study the track he was on – it was rugged, not that well-kept, boggy in parts. Water certainly wasn't in short supply in this area of Scotland. That was one reason perhaps that people didn't see the need to gather together in villages. The residents of Anwoth didn't think it was essential to congregate around a well or a loch like they did in other parts of the country. They just set up their homesteads where the land was most fertile. This made sense even if it meant a long journey to the next farm. Fertile land for crop growing wasn't always conveniently placed. Samuel supposed that it was a blessing to have such ready access to water for drinking and bathing, but when it was dripping down the back of your neck it wasn't so pleasant. He shivered and rubbed his arms to get the blood flowing. It would be good to get into a warm, dry house.

The wind felt so bitterly cold Samuel could hardly believe that it was spring, but it said so on the calendar and on the dates of the several letters he had sent by post before he left Edinburgh. There were young lambs bleating within earshot. 'No doubt they are complaining to their mothers about this terrible cold,' Samuel thought to himself as he dismounted in order to get his bearings once again.

'There must be farms around here somewhere,' he muttered, 'the animals prove that. The shepherd can't be that far away.' But he could not see a solitary human being, not even a trail of smoke from a chimney.

'I must be some distance from Anwoth still,' Samuel grimaced. Dark clouds loomed behind him – it seemed that worse weather was chasing the pastor, and at some speed. He could mount his horse again and force the tired animal to charge up the hill. But even the threat of a fierce snowstorm couldn't bring Samuel to treat the tired beast in such a way. The horse deserved a rest. The least Samuel could do now was keep his feet on the ground. He spoke gently to his dappled grey as he stroked its soft cheeks and tussled mane, 'We'll walk up this next hill together. I won't make you carry me until we are on the downward slope once more. My books, pens, papers and other items are enough of a burden for you on such a steep climb.'

The horse nuzzled his master's shoulder knowing that somewhere within that damp and windswept cape was an apple. 'Not yet,' Samuel urged. 'We've got to arrive at Anwoth before nightfall. And you can see the storm too. There's no more time for apples and treats. We need to get going. I want to be in our new home[2] when it is still light enough to see and I think I can taste snow in the air.'

---

2. In many publications you will see the Rutherford's home referred to as Bush-O' Bield. This was the name given to the home of Samuel and Eupham Rutherford in Anwoth probably after they lived in it.

Moving forward he wrapped his long cape tighter. Step after step after step he urged himself and his horse up the hill. It was a far cry from the cobbled streets of the capital city. 'Hopefully everything will all be dryer and less slippery by next week.' Samuel was concerned for his wife and child and the journey they would take to join him. The cart might make it alright if the road was less boggy, a carriage would have difficulty.

More used to sitting in a lecture theatre than walking the hills, Samuel found the steep climb a struggle. His muscles burned with the strain. However, although his muscles burned, his feet were frozen! Everything, even his robes were considerably damper by the time he reached the top of the hill.

'At last,' he called out 'it can't be far now.'

Taking a pen knife out of his pocket, he cut a small piece off an apple and fed it to his eager mount. As the horse ate its treat Samuel Rutherford scanned the horizon. The clouds were closer, the sun was lower and there, several miles south of where he stood, he spotted a thin line of blue-grey smoke meandering above what appeared to be a grove or two of trees.

'That must be Anwoth,' Samuel supposed. The beginning of his new life – and a new life for his wife, Eupham, and their young child.

'I am to be the new minister of this new parish,' Samuel thought to himself as he placed his foot in the stirrup and hauled himself back up into the saddle. 'I

Samuel Rutherford

hope Eupham and the bairn[3] will settle well in this far away place. It is a great change for me but even greater for them. So many new things in such a short space of time.' He spoke to himself, simply to hear a human voice in this great empty space. It was a small comfort.

Anwoth was to be his first charge as a minister, but it was also the first time that Anwoth had had a minister and church of their own. There had never been a ministry in this area before. In the past it had always been tagged on to another parish. 'I'm turning a new page in my life as are the people who live here,' Samuel acknowledged. 'I suppose I'm feeling somewhat excited but I'm worried too.' Samuel frowned. He was just the sort of person who could swing from being positively positive to being downright negative at the drop of a hat. Ups and downs would always be a part of his life and ministry.

Today Samuel was betwixt many different emotions – missing his wife and child but longing for a warm hearth. He looked back with fondness on the life he had left behind, but he also anticipated with eagerness the new experiences to come. But what were they going to be exactly? Samuel wasn't sure about the answer to that question.

For one thing Samuel didn't really know how to look after a congregation. Writing sermons and preaching – he thought he would enjoy that but what about the

---

3. Scotland has a different vocabulary that is often referred to as 'broad scots.' Bairn is a broad scots word for child.

The Law, the Prince and the Scribe

other responsibilities of the task – of those he wasn't so sure. However, with the Lord God's help he would learn them, of that he was certain.

One of the things that he would have to learn would be where everyone was. Looking north, south, east and west there were miles upon miles of rolling hills. Samuel realised that his life as a pastor would involve getting to know these rough roads and perilous uplands considerably well. There would be many cottages that he would have to visit in order to teach and care for the souls of the area.

'You'll be trotting through these empty spaces with me,' he said to the now rested horse. 'I'll know them as well as your hooves and my hands before too long.' At that Samuel spotted that the sun had descended even more and would soon begin to disappear behind the high ridge. A snowflake landed on his eyelash and Samuel briskly brushed it away, 'Get on now, old friend,' Samuel urged. 'There should be a warm welcome waiting for us at the manse.' The chimney smoke in the distance was most likely the house they were headed for.

The horse shook its mane and sped up from a walk to a trot. Within the hour they were near enough to the smoking chimney to smell the aroma of burning logs and to see that, indeed, the manor house they were approaching was the church manse, the building set aside to be the minister's home. This would be where the Rutherford family would settle as soon as Eupham and the child arrived. As the building came into focus Samuel also spotted two elderly people waving at him from the side of the road. Large holly bushes sheltered the building from the front. Pine and ash trees grew in the adjoining pastures.

The old man waved his cap eagerly as he called out to Samuel, 'Come away in.' The old woman had gathered up her skirts to run back to the house – no doubt she would soon be at the large open hearth warming through some soup. Samuel dismounted and shook hands eagerly with his welcomer. 'At last,' Samuel exclaimed. 'I meet some of my congregation.'

'So, you do Mr Rutherford, so you do. And we're that glad to see you, our own minister. Come into the warmth before you catch a chill,' the old man urged. He made as if he would take the horse from him, but Samuel wanted to settle his mount himself.

'I will come in,' Samuel agreed, 'once I have housed my horse in the stable. 'I'll see to his needs first and then to mine. But come with me and show me where things are kept.'

'Yes – yes,' the old man said, shuffling along the path as Samuel followed, 'the stables are here to the back with everything you need for your animal. It won't take us long to settle him in his new lodgings. Then we'll take your things inside and get you fed and watered. The two of you must be fair exhausted after such a journey. And you've made it just in time.' The old man cast a wary eye to the heavens. 'It's going to be bitterly cold tonight. There's a grand sky full of snow up there, but the fire is on in your bedroom good and strong.'

The Law, the Prince and the Scribe

Samuel breathed a sigh of relief at the thought of a warm bed, a warm fire and some warm food. He supposed that even the king himself could not want for anything more on such a night as this.

With the horse fed and comfortable Samuel himself was looked after. The thick soup and crusty bread, with local farm-made cheese, were soon being devoured by the hungry traveller. Samuel hadn't realised how famished he was. The cheese was as delicious as any he had ever tasted. 'It must be because it is so fresh.' Food straight from the farm would be a healthy way to feed his children he reckoned. And most of the tenant farms in these parts would have at least one dairy cow to provide milk, cheese and butter. Perhaps even a goat or two. In Edinburgh you were likely to live next door to a lawyer or notary. Maybe a seamstress or a shoemaker. There were many different trades; people who sold you what you needed when you wanted new clothes or footwear. In the agricultural communities, like Anwoth, your neighbours were people of the soil. They grew what they ate and made what they wore. They even crafted soap and candles from what was left over after they had butchered their animals. It was, on the whole, a self-reliant community. However, Samuel sincerely hoped that these people would also come to rely on God in this life and for the life to come[4].

---

4. Life to Come: this is a phrase that was and is still used today to describe heaven or eternity.

Samuel Rutherford

Samuel picked out from a drawer one of those candles purchased from a nearby cottage. It was time for him to go to bed. As he made his way up the stairs he paused at a window – it was pitch dark outside except for a thin slither of moon. The light of the candle flame helped him to see what could be a small vegetable patch and a honeysuckle bush. Samuel was sure he had caught the scent of one as he had left the stable earlier. A little draught made the candle flicker, so he shielded it with his hand to ensure it didn't blow out. There wasn't much else that he could see at this time of night – perhaps that was a shadow of another building, probably the church. A dim light in the distance could be a peasant's cottage. Tomorrow he would do his best to explore the area.

As for the house, it was a good-sized building that had belonged at one point to some people who were well off, perhaps landowners or merchants. There were lots of rooms, far more than the Rutherfords needed. Samuel wondered about closing some to save on heating. Two or three bedrooms were all they would require, perhaps a dining room and a parlour and then Samuel remembered that a minister needed a study – something with enough room for all the books that would be arriving with his wife the following week.

As he turned down the covers that night, he was thankful that they had a house, that soon they would call this building home and one day, hoped Samuel, the people of Anwoth would be as dear as family to them.

The Law, the Prince and the Scribe

Samuel was eager to start writing about all the new experiences of the day, the impressions that he had gleaned of his brief time in Anwoth. Perhaps a quick letter tomorrow to Eupham would be helpful, so she would know what to expect. But then maybe it was best just to let her make her own mind up about the place. The letter probably wouldn't get to Edinburgh in time anyway.

Kneeling by the bed his last words were a prayer to his Lord God. 'My eternal God and Heavenly Father, you have sent me here to preach salvation, to preach about you and what you have done for my soul. You have sent me to preach the good news of your Son to the people of this fair town of Anwoth. May I fasten my hold firmly upon Christ and esteem you my richest possession. My helper and strength. Amen Lord Jesus.'

And with that he closed his eyes in rest. It was one of his greatest joys to spend his last moments before sleep thinking about his Saviour. Almost every night since he had been saved, the name of Jesus Christ was the last name he spoke of before his eyes closed.

Songbirds by the Solway

The following morning Samuel woke early with the songbirds, as was his custom. He made it a personal habit to go to bed in good time and to get up early to pray and meditate on the Word of God. His Bible was the first book he pulled out of his saddle bag. He had left it beside his bed the previous night. There were a few books that he just couldn't leave behind in Edinburgh. He had to have his Bible and the other titles that were needed for the sermon he planned to preach on the Lord's Day. More books would arrive with his wife and child, who would follow shortly with what little furniture they possessed. Samuel didn't own much in the way of this world's goods, so, for now, the manse looked a bit empty. However, he didn't really mind as all that the young pastor needed was a chair, a small table and a candle. All three were conveniently placed in the corner of his room. What more did one man need?

The manse and its surroundings were the perfect environment for prayer and thought.

The Law, the Prince and the Scribe

So, he bowed his head to speak to his Lord and Saviour as he had done on many mornings since he had first come to faith in Christ.

As he raised his head from prayer, some time later, the little songbird was still in strong voice, but there was another sound in the background. 'I think I can hear a stream running through the garden,' Samuel thought. The rush and gurgle were vigorous and told Samuel, without his even looking, that the fresh fall of snow was now filling the local waterways. Splashing and crashing over the rocks, thundering its way towards the Solway Firth not that far away.

The sound of doors opening and closing on the floor below told Samuel that the local help had arrived. The woman, dressed in an apron with her hair tied tight in a bun, was already in the kitchen when Samuel came downstairs. She looked up startled at the sight of the minister out of bed so early. Samuel smiled. 'I'm glad to see that there's someone else awake with the larks. It's often that I come downstairs in the morning and there's not a soul to talk to.'

The woman welcomed him and quickly had a pan of porridge over the kitchen fire. Samuel insisted on eating this with her in the kitchen. 'There's no point in using the dining room when it's just me in the house. And besides I've got some questions to ask you. You're a local and I've never stepped foot in this area before. I've not seen the church building itself yet.'

Samuel Rutherford

'Well, it's not far,' the woman waved her wash cloth towards the back door. 'There's a short walk bordered by trees between the manse and the church building.'

Samuel nodded, 'After breakfast I'll go exploring, perhaps when the sun is a bit higher in the sky. Fresh air and a bit of exercise – that will do me good.'

Even though he had spent days in the saddle with enough fresh air for a lifetime, Samuel still insisted on a regular routine. Exercise was just another of Rutherford's regular habits. His was a disciplined life, but it was also a creative one. The papers and notes in his study were testament to that.

If you picked up one of his letters[1] you would read some heartfelt descriptive lines particularly written to comfort or encourage a person in exactly the trouble or challenge that they found themselves in. Notes for his sermons were like poetry. Then there were the deeper, more thought-provoking articles. The papers around his desk showed that here was a man who liked to think and think deeply. He cared about his soul, his church, the people and his world. There was no person too poor or lowly to whom he would not reach out. But there was also no monarch or ruler so great that he would not engage with.

For now, all those notes and papers were neatly tied up in the other saddle bag that was hanging on

---

1. Charles Spurgeon once said of Samuel Rutherford's Letters: 'When we are dead and gone let the world know that Spurgeon held Rutherford's letters to be the nearest thing to inspiration which can be found in all the writings of mere men.'

the peg of his bedroom door. Some of them he would send off into the world to houses and homes of friends and family. Other passages that he had written were thoughts and questions he was working through. These would not see the world quite as quickly as his letters, but the effect they would have would be rather considerable.

Samuel continued his conversation with the maid as she cleared the kitchen and got ready for the rest of her day. He asked her questions about the local people, who he should visit first. Were there any people sick and housebound and what was the best route to get to this or that cottager? The answers to these questions were promptly answered and before too long Samuel had made a mental note of the first few people he would seek out. His horse would have a well-earned rest for a day or two, building up its energy in a warm dry stable, before stretching its legs in the paddock. But the following week would involve some hiking, as the two of them would ride out to visit the parish. 'Mr Wilson, with his injured back, lives beyond the Grey's farm. Mrs Nicholson can't come to church on the Lord's Day on account of her eyesight and bad leg.' These were just two names the maid had mentioned who would need the minister's care and assistance.

Rutherford retired to his room to do some final unpacking and then before lunch he set off to find the church. The snow from the previous day was sitting in pockets and gullies but already it had started to melt a little. It seemed to Samuel that this sudden blast of winter wouldn't last too long and perhaps it would be the final fall of the year. Samuel was certain that the farmers would be glad if that was the case. As he started towards the church, he cast his eye across the horizon. In the distance he heard the unmistakable call of a shepherd and the bark of his dog as they worked the flock. It was good to be amongst farming people again. Although Samuel had spent most of the last few years in the big city, he was familiar with country folk and their ways as he had grown up on a farm of sorts.

His father's people had owned land and lived in and around the village of Nisbet near Jedburgh. They hadn't been poor like many tenant farmers – they had in fact been rich enough to send their three sons to school and get a university education for Samuel.

His parents had made considerable sacrifices for the education of the three Rutherford boys – Samuel, George and James. George had gone into teaching. James was now serving in the military, but Samuel had been the one with the talent. After his graduation he had been accepted as a professor of Humanities at the prestigious Edinburgh University. It was quite the accolade for a farmer's son from the Borders, but he had never forgotten his roots. Samuel had fond memories of being a country lad, walking through the hills, playing and fishing by the river. He loved his strolls amongst nature, being with people who worked the land. Anwoth would be very similar to the place of his birth, Samuel reckoned.

'There will be one difference,' Samuel hoped. 'I trust that the gospel will be preached here and that Jesus will be spoken of with love and joy. My memory of Nisbet is that very few spoke of Christ.'

Nisbet hadn't been devoid of godly people, but Christ was not someone they ever really talked about. The fact is, if you want to find out what someone cares about most then you should listen to their conversations. You'll soon discover what their passions are. Samuel realised that the gospel had not been a passion of his hometown because praise of Christ had hardly ever crossed anyone's lips. Had it not been for one godly pastor, Samuel would have had little Christian influence outside of his family. The godly pastor, however, had been kicked out of his charge because of his Presbyterian[2] beliefs. So, the Nisbet that Rutherford knew had faced spiritual poverty. Samuel didn't want that to happen in Anwoth. He didn't want the young of this parish to be as he once was – paying no regard to their souls and their need of salvation.

The sun was at its height now as Samuel stood before the church building. He would preach the gospel of Christ here on the Lord's Day – but the preciousness

---

2. Presbyterian: This word applies to churches that follow the teachings of John Calvin and John Knox and practice a presbyterian form of church government led by representative elders (presbyters). Local congregations elect a board called the session and elect presbyters who form a presbytery to govern groups of local churches. Presbyteries are overseen by synods, and the synods together form the General Assembly.

of Christ and salvation had been totally lost to him in his earlier days. As he opened the door, he let his mind drift back. Those memories brought a blush of shame to his cheeks. Samuel felt he had been so foolish to delay coming to Christ. He had behaved like someone who was waiting for the sun to be high in the sky before they ventured out in the fresh air. However, Samuel knew that the best time to go on a walk was early in the morning. It would have been far better if Samuel had followed Jesus early in his life, instead Samuel had dithered and delayed his decision to trust in Jesus. Thankfully, Jesus had never delayed in loving Him.

He cast his eye over the pews before him. They would easily seat at least 200 he reckoned. Samuel remembered with joy how Christ, his Saviour, had forgiven him. As he looked around the church some more, Samuel thought, *'Christ has a saving eye. When he first looked on me, I was saved. It cost him but a look to make hell quit to me.'*

And quit it had. Samuel knew and believed with certainty that God had saved him from hell and eternal punishment and that everlasting life was his. Death and hell now held no power. Those days were gone – the days when he had little regard for Christ and his need of salvation. Now his days were filled with a passion for the lost sinner. He was called to preach the Good News of Christ to these needy souls. It had not been that long ago when he had been just like them - without Christ and without hope.

The Law, the Prince and the Scribe

Samuel looked at the uncluttered architecture of the building with its oak pulpit and open Bible in pride of place. An oval window at the back let sunbeams pick out the simplicity of the communion table and pews. He imagined what this place would look like with people in it worshipping simply, the way God's Word commanded. Heads bowed in prayer, voices raised in praise, hearts open to God's Holy Spirit. Two galleries were at either end of the church. Samuel noted them both with interest. Those areas were reserved for the two noble families, the Lennoxes of Cally and the Gordons of Cardoness and Rusco. But when it came to the Kingdom of God, Samuel acknowledged that earthly position meant nothing. In the church of Christ, the peasant and the pauper could take the same communion bread and wine as the Lord and the Lady. The clean white linen on the table was spread out for rich and poor alike, when they remembered the sacrifice of Christ on the cross.

Samuel sat down at the edge of one of the wooden pews. Resting his head in his hands he let out a sigh. Looking up to the pulpit in front of him his heart felt heavy. Was he worthy of this calling? It was at least a year now, but the shame felt like yesterday. The University of Edinburgh had thrown him out. He had left the academic world under a cloud. Some called it a scandal. Was it his fault? Yes, maybe no. Could he have done things differently? No, maybe yes.

It was his marriage to Eupham that they used to remove him from his charge. Were all these accusations just or fair? Had there been something inappropriate about their relationship? Samuel knew the private temptations of his heart. And although he understood that there was no real accusation, fault or blame to be laid at his door – he wasn't totally free of guilt. As he bowed his head in the silence of the kirk[3], he shared his private grief with the only one who knew him completely. There was no one else but God beside him in the pew to listen to his repentance.

At least everything was in the open. He had willingly resigned his position so that there would be no prolonged bitter enmity between him and the faculty[4]. And in the end, everyone had just gone on as usual. His accusers never brought up the issue again and they were quite willing to let the young man go on to study theology and become a preacher. Though Samuel felt some grief about his actions it was obvious that he hadn't really done anything that shocking. But the 1600s was a strange time. Monarchs were allowed to do what they liked when a humble professor wasn't even allowed to get married without university permission.

Samuel's decision to leave the world of classes and lectures meant he now found himself in the world of the preacher – a world that was God's choice for Samuel, so it was the best choice. 'I may have my doubts about myself but not about my Lord and His Word. And it is

---

3. Kirk – broad Scots word for Church.
4. Faculty: A group of university departments connected to a particular subject.

The Law, the Prince and the Scribe

clear that God's call is that I should preach that Word to His flock.'

So as Samuel raised his head from prayer, he ended his conversation with God in deep thanks. The difficult situation that he and Eupham had found themselves in now meant that they were where God meant them to be – as husband, wife, mother, father – and now pastor and pastor's wife.

With that, he rose from the pew and began to make his way towards the pulpit.

At about the same time as his troubles at university had begun Samuel's heart had been won by Christ. And this whole experience had drawn him afresh to the Word of God, while also re-igniting his conviction that the people of the church should make the decisions in the church alongside God's Word.

That was one of the unique characteristics of being a Presbyterian and Scotland had been Presbyterian since the Reformation and John Knox, in the previous century. However, James VI had forced the nation and the Church of Scotland to adopt Episcopacy[5] and Roman Catholic practices. And that had been the beginning of years of bitter conflict between the throne, the church and the people.

The fact that Samuel had never supported the Episcopalian system may have been the real reason

---

5. Episcopacy: This is the system of church government in which bishops are established as superior to priests or presbyters. Instead of local congregations choosing their own minister in the episcopal system bishops often made these decisions and not the people.

Samuel Rutherford

people wanted him out of Edinburgh University. Perhaps a more cunning man would have weathered the storms better. Samuel's support of Presbyterianism hadn't won any champions to his corner. However, as Samuel climbed the stairs of the pulpit, he once again hung his head. Regrets would never be far away from him, even when he was experiencing hope and joy he would remember his past. '*The old ashes of the sins of my youth are a new fire of sorrow to me*'.

But preaching the Word of God was a blessed opportunity and it thrilled and humbled him in equal measure. 'I may be hidden in the backwoods of the country, miles from anywhere but that's not such a bad place to be,' he reminded himself, 'especially as Anwoth is where I believe God means me to be for His glory.'

Walking back to the manse, he raised his eyes to the heavens again. The scent of pine was in the air and a beautiful little blue-winged bird flitted this way and that along the pathway, singing its heart out. Samuel felt as though he should join in and sang a Psalm of praise to God as he made his way home.

Always Writing, Always Preaching

It didn't take long before Samuel got into his stride as the minister of Anwoth. His daily practices and habits soon became an interesting topic of conversation among the people of the area. There wasn't a village as such because Anwoth was more a far-flung collection of houses and hearths than streets and squares. However, the locals could still witness the daily habits of their minister as he went about his day and they went about theirs. And whenever they met each other, the minister ended up as a topic of conversation.

'I saw him crossing the burn this morning as quick as you like on his way to the Howat's no doubt. The bairns there all have a fever, and nobody's been able to come to the kirk for weeks.'

'He was visiting Mrs Fraser the day before last. She lost her husband not so long ago. His visits are a great comfort to the poor soul.'

'He always has a book or something with him on his travels. The maid says the papers on his desk are so many she dare not touch them in case they end up in

The Law, the Prince and the Scribe

the wrong order. The pastor sits and writes for hours most days.'

'Does he indeed? A regular scribe then. I've heard from Mr Ross that the candle is burning in that study window as early as three in the morning.'

'Mr Ross is up at that time?'

'Well, not as a rule, but their new baby is teething,' and with that the conversation changed to what the best remedy was for sore gums, and sleepless nights.

These were also problems in the Rutherford house on occasion, now that there were two children to look after. Eupham had given birth to another baby, and there was a toddler running around the manse. Samuel's life as a young father was busy and hectic as the lives of many fathers are. But he was a pastor so had two families to look after – his home family and his church family, and these co-existed in a world that was more than usually problematic. The 1600s was a difficult century to be part of. It was harsh and what you and I think of as every-day items were unthought of luxuries for those people. Yet, it was an exciting time to be alive. Samuel would have made sure he was kept informed of what was going on in the world around him. And what a world it was. Samuel shared the same century as William Shakespeare, the Pilgrim Fathers and the Gunpowder Plot.[1] There was a lot going on!

---

1. William Shakespeare was a playwright who wrote Romeo and Juliet. The Pilgrim Fathers were the first settlers in America. Gunpowder Plot this was a failed assassination attempt against King James VI.

Samuel Rutherford

Samuel was only three years-old when the great monarch Queen Elizabeth I died, and King James of Scotland inherited her crown. Mary Queen of Scots had been his mother. So both he and Elizabeth were descendants of King Henry VIII. When James succeeded to Elizabeth's throne, Scotland and England were united under one crown or ruler. They were still separate in some ways. Both nations had their own church, parliament and legal system. But Scotland was also Presbyterian and the people of England worshipped in the Church of England – under an Episcopalian form of church government. Under the English system, the monarch was head of the church and bishops appointed by the monarch made all the decisions, even who would preach and where. King James was adamant that Scotland should also adopt the same form of church that England had. This would mean he would have the same powers in his native land as he had in his new realm.

In England the people and congregations had little if any say in government or in spiritual matters. Scotland soon became the same. Many, like Rutherford, strongly disagreed with this.

Although occasionally the lit candle in the window at the manse meant a fractious child was not cooperating – more often it meant that Samuel Rutherford was praying or reading or writing. Sometimes he was just thinking. In the violent and turbulent 1600s there was a lot to think about. Samuel thought long and hard about something called the divine right of kings. Monarchs like James VI and his descendants believed that God had put them in charge and that because of that they could do anything they wished – even if that meant disobeying God's law.

Did they indeed have the right to do what they wanted? Had God really put them in charge to such an extent that even if they disobeyed God's law they couldn't be touched? Samuel Rutherford was adamant that the answers to those questions was no. And what Samuel thought about he also wrote about and, as time went on, there were a lot of papers on the desk of the Anwoth pastor. People in his congregation, and friends that knew him well, would describe Samuel Rutherford as 'always praying, always reading, always writing, always preaching ...' He was always at the work!

The most important part of the work as far as Samuel was concerned, was preaching. That was where his heart lay, and his congregation loved him for this. They knew they had a good man in Rutherford. He had come to their parish under strong recommendations, but it was the congregation themselves who decided for Rutherford and called him to be their preacher. Even though the Church of Scotland was now being run by bishops, it seemed that some parishes still operated under the old ways – and did their own thing. Samuel Rutherford was known as a Presbyterian and Anwoth apparently was very happy to have a Presbyterian in the pulpit.

The very fact that he preached twice on the Lord's Day was enough to prove to the locals they had made the right choice. Having two sermons to listen to was something entirely new and a true treasure trove of spiritual blessings. For many years they'd only had one sermon every second week because there wasn't a church in Anwoth. Those who could tried their best to travel to a neighbouring parish, but this was quite a distance and certainly not something that the elderly could manage or young families. To only have the occasional sermon was described by some of the people in Anwoth as a 'famine'. But now they had their own minister they were enjoying two sermons a week! It was a feast! And the sermons he preached fully satisfied the Christians! Not only that – the conversations Rutherford had with them at the spinning wheel or in the barn, showed the people of Anwoth that they had a minister with a heart for their souls. He wasn't one of those men who rushed out a few words and a psalm and then left the pulpit until the following week. Rutherford could be seen at work – on his knees, in his Bible, in the homes.

The peasants and farmers, as well as the gentry and landowners, all enjoyed his preaching. Whenever they listened to him, they heard about Christ's love, Christ's faithfulness, Christ's salvation. These sermons were so rich with Christ that over the years people began to travel to Anwoth from a considerable distance simply to hear Samuel for themselves. There were folk in other areas that didn't have their own minister or didn't have a minister who preached the gospel. Men and women who longed to hear the Bible explained to them, to hear of the love of Christ, salvation, the forgiveness of sins, didn't mind the long journey to Anwoth.

Some individuals though didn't like the fact that he was so popular. They couldn't stand the fact that Samuel was noticeably a Presbyterian. One of those was Thomas Sydserf the Bishop of Galloway. He began to find Samuel Rutherford more than just a bit annoying and began to plot how he could make Samuel's life difficult. Samuel pushed back against the increasing influence of the episcopal church and the fact that Roman Catholic traditions were once again gaining acceptance. He preached against it and he preached the truth — the truth that sinners needed to be saved and saved through the blood of Christ, not through doing good works, or paying money to the church.

When walking about the area he would often keep an eye out for examples of ordinary things that could illustrate godly truths. Moments from his day would often jump out at him and become the perfect sermon illustration or final paragraph in a pastoral letter.

His own children could easily supply what was needed. A stumbling little toddler in the kitchen trying to hold two apples in her hand was quite an amusing sight. Samuel picked up one as she dropped it and reminded himself to write down the experience when he went to his study.

'Just as a child cannot hold two apples in one hand neither can we have two masters or Lords in our life — we cannot serve

the world and Christ. ... We must fasten our hold firmly on Jesus Christ. We must look on Him as our richest possession.'

One thing that Samuel's congregation often noticed about their preacher was how frequent his walks were. Not only did he cross the hills and valleys to visit with the people of his congregation, he often took a stroll in the fresh air along the little path that stretched from the manse to the church. It didn't take long for the people of Anwoth to call that stretch of road, 'Rutherford's Walk'.

On these walks he would often be seen looking to the sky – what he was looking at, nobody was sure. But it was clear that during his walks he enjoyed spending time with God and with nature. 'Perhaps he can see something of heaven in his surroundings that we simply can't,' one old gentleman guessed as he saw his pastor disappear into the pine trees. 'Looking at nature does seem to make him think of the Creator.'

The seasons of nature were, in fact, a great source of inspiration for Samuel. He loved to look at the birds flying around the manse or church. Depending on what time of year it was, there would be different colours of wing, flitting here and there. Songbirds making their voices heard in the spring. Swallows soaring in the summer, making their nests under the eaves of the church. The flowers of the manse garden delighted him with their scent and beauty and even these little nuggets of nature would bring him spiritual strength. The aroma of their petals would remind him of how the love of Jesus Christ was as rich and intense as a blossoming rose.

'God has made many flowers but the greatest of all flowers is in heaven, our Lord Jesus Christ.'

Samuel's thoughts and inspiration came from good weather and bad. When the season of flowers was over, icy blasts gave Samuel inspiration too – particularly about the dangers of sin.

Early one winter before the really big blizzards had arrived, he was called on to visit an elderly member of his congregation. The journey had started off fair but had changed for the worse in a sudden and terrifying way. Dark clouds loomed on the horizon and soon Samuel realised that a vicious storm was about to wreak havoc on the hillside. He was too far along his route to turn back, so Samuel made the decision to press on. When bending his shoulders against the storm he found himself struggling to advance even a step. The temperature was dropping, the snow was beginning to fall and with every step forward he found with the next gust of wind he had to take two steps back. As he fought on, he remembered the words of Scripture that said how easy it was for sin to strike us. Sin was very much like this storm he was facing.

'Sin can hinder us from hearing God's Word, from praying. It can even stop us believing. Stop us hoping.' Another blast of wind almost swept him off his feet. He struggled to keep his foothold on the slippery path. More snow wound its way around him, obscuring his vision and as

Samuel Rutherford

the sky darkened Samuel began to feel a slight panic in his breast. *'Sin can darken your life as this storm is darkening my sight. It can take away sound judgment, causing a person to make the wrong choice, take the wrong path,' he thought.* But just then the sound of a dog barking in the distance brought relief to Samuel's heart and he soon found his way to the warm hearth he had been searching for.

'It's not a good day to be out and about, minister,' the old farmer admonished. He was delighted that Rutherford had taken the trouble to visit him in such weather but wasn't sure about the wisdom of the pastor's actions. It certainly was a blessing to have a preacher who was as committed to his flock as Rutherford was. Not many men would make the effort to visit their congregations when it was raining, far less in a winter storm. 'But all the better for me,' thought the host.' I'll get some good company and conversation to be sure.'

And Samuel enjoyed the company too. There was warmth, simple food, and a blazing fire. The storm howling outside couldn't touch him. Eventually, the panic in his breast subsided as he sat down to wait out the bad weather.

Samuel had been in many houses, grand ones at that. In his Edinburgh days he would be hosted by faculty and rich nobles. Even in Anwoth Samuel was acquainted with people like the Gordons who lived at Rusco Castle. He often wrote letters to them and was confident that some were loyal to the cause of Christ.

The Law, the Prince and the Scribe

However, landed gentry with all their riches were no richer in conversation or spiritual insight than many a poor shepherd or farmer.

The conversations he had with a man who knew what it was like to till the land or care for sheep, would often bring to Samuel's mind portions of Scripture, words of wisdom that he would then share with others. The man who ploughed his land in the autumn and then waited on the spring to sow his seed, before harvesting the oats with his scythe in the summer, showed great patience. Samuel thought more about this as he waved goodbye to his country host. The storm was over, and Samuel realised that he had been more than a bit impatient as he had waited for the wild weather to pass. The farmer and men like him lived in a world where you had to be patient about everything. Impatience got you nowhere. 'But who is it that shows the most patience?' Samuel pondered. The answer to that was simple.

'*What is our patience,*' Samuel declared '*compared to Christ's? He has shown so much patience with me in my life. He shows such patience with His church. He is like a loving husband and we, His people, are like His cherished bride.*'

Picking up his step he hurried home to his own wife and children, anxious that they would have no cause to worry about him and his adventures. However, it wasn't long before once again Samuel was thinking about who he would visit next from his 'dear flock' in Anwoth.

Set Your Arrow Straight

Just as any flock has sheep and lambs, so Samuel's congregation had people young and old. And although he was concerned about everyone in the parish, whatever age they were, Samuel had a particular concern for the young people of the area. He devised his own catechism – a series of questions and answers that would help the children he met with learn about God's Word and God's character. When he visited the different houses and families in the area he would sit down with the younger members of these homes and ask them the questions. They would do their best to give the right answers and were particularly pleased when they got a smile and a pat on the back from their minister.

However, Samuel was also concerned about the young men of the parish. He found it a great burden to see how little they cared for the Word of God or for following His commands. The Lord's Day was not held in special regard and he frequently saw lads kicking a football about when they should have been in church. He would do his best to gently reprimand them. Disappointingly, it often had little effect. So, he would have to leave them with a warning for their souls.

There were some young men who did attend the church services. They appeared to listen, while with others it was clear they wanted to be anywhere but in the Lord's House. Samuel realised that he had to speak to them in their language, about things they understood so that they could also understand God's Word.

Returning from Rutherford Walk one afternoon, he saw in the distance a lad of about fourteen or fifteen years of age. He was quietly making his way through a patch of woodland with a bow and arrow in his grasp.

'He must be hunting for something,' Samuel pondered. And yes, he was. The young man stopped in his tracks, his eye fixed, his body tense. He slowly stretched the string with the arrow head sitting tight and snug waiting to be released. Suddenly he let it fly, and everything happened in a blur. Samuel heard the twang of the bow and then the thud as the arrow hit its target – a particularly plump partridge had not been paying attention.

'That will give his family a good meal for the table,' Samuel smiled. 'He is a young man with a good aim. If he had not spent the time fixing his eye and setting the arrow he could easily have missed that bird.' Samuel felt the beginnings of a story. 'Here again is something that I must tell the young people.'

Samuel spent the next few hours stitching together his thoughts, making a picture that any young man would be able to see in his mind. *'It is easy to master an arrow and set it right before the string is drawn. But once you have shot it and it is in the air it is a different matter. Once the arrow begins to fly you have no control over it. Your thoughts and affections are just like arrows. You must have them under God's control. Your love must be aimed towards Christ. Make Him the centre of your aim and your desire. When you give away your affections you will not have the power to take them back. Once the arrow is shot you cannot make it return.'*

Samuel had seen so many young men waste their lives on worldly things rather than give their love to Christ. They preferred to play sport, and drink alcohol. They would rather exhaust themselves making their way to a dance than break a sweat walking to church.

Samuel longed for the young men who sat before him in church to take God's Word to heart so that it would change their lives. Again, he remembered his own young life and how he had fallen into temptations that he deeply regretted to this day.

He prayed passionately that he would see hearts won to Christ. Although there were believers in his congregation, he was not seeing many sinners come to Christ under his ministry.

'My congregation must hear the gospel, they must be told that salvation is offered to them freely. Christ is coming to everyone with good news. So, there is no one who has an excuse. Everyone is obliged to believe in the power of Christ's infinite mercy. Some people think that they can refuse Christ's mercy and forgiveness because you have to be ready to become

a Christian. I need to make it clear to them that salvation is not just for sinners who are convicted of their sin or who are seeking salvation. When people think like that it is of the devil.'

Although Samuel was uncertain about whether people were listening to his sermons, or being brought to Christ, believers *were* being spiritually fed and they rejoiced to hear him speak about Christ and the cross. The preacher's words *were* powerful. He would personally and passionately plead with his people to repent and come to Christ. He would remind the young and the old of Anwoth that they were 'Christ's bairns' and that just as bairns (children) came to their mothers and fathers for food to fill their bellies the believers of Anwoth were to come to God's Word for their spiritual food.

Samuel made a point of saying, firmly, *'It is Christ's will that His bairns get their fill and that they grow. Christ never had a hungry house, nor His Father before Him. There is bread and drink in God's house. Eat and drink, for it will do you good. You get it with Christ's good will, and with His heartsome blessing. Now in the strength of it work a good work to Christ, your Master. Do you know Christ beloved? He kens (knows) you full well. Come near Him and stand not afar off. Christ says look on me whom you have pierced with your sins. You must not turn your shoulder to Christ but set your face toward Him. Take home the king's pardon with you, written in your Lord's own heart blood.'*

Samuel's words may sound slightly strange to us. They spoke and wrote differently in times gone by,

Samuel Rutherford

but as well as that Samuel was a romantic. This showed in his vocabulary as he spilled out poetry with every breath.

Samuel urged believers in his congregation and elsewhere not to sit back and relax in the Christian life but to be active and at work.

'Christ has fed you to run a race, even a race to heaven. Christ now takes you into the chariot with Him and draws your hearts after Him. Don't be Satan's footmen any longer, for it is a wearisome life. But ride with Christ in His chariot for it is filled with love. It is better to be Christ's horsemen and ride than to be Satan's trogged (dirty) footmen. Christ has washed you so sin no more. Take you to Christ, the fairest of ten thousand. When Christ was black and blae (blue) upon the cross and pale with death He was then fairest.'[1]

The pastor, who was always in his books, who had come from one of the greatest universities in the land and who spoke and read fluent Latin was not ashamed to use the tongue of the ordinary working people in his sermons.

Words like *bairns, trogged*, and *ken* – were all Scots words. The local people had their own vocabulary, their own heart language and Samuel used it with skill to teach them about the love of Christ. The natives of Scotland even had their own word for church. They used the word *Kirk*. And whenever they came to hear their minister preach in their *Kirk*, they heard the

---

1. These words were recorded from a sermon preached to a Scots congregation in London in 1643, during the Westminster Assembly.

simple gospel in words that they not only understood but used themselves.

'*Christ would coss* (barter) *lives with you and make a niffer* (exchange). *He took shame and gave you glory. He took the curse and gave you the blessing. He took death and gave you life. The fairest candle that ever was lighted was blown out. But our Lord Jesus was aye to be lippened* (trusted). *What do you think of Christ? Is not He fair and lovely? He is altogether lovely. Christ took a hearty grip of you upon the cross. He will not let you slip out of His fingers.*

They tied thieves bands'[2] to the hands of our Saviour, hands that had never stolen, that had never shed blood. Bands bound His hands, but love, mercy and grace bound His tender heart with stronger bands and cords – to free us out of the bands of sin. He cried in the Spirit, 'Father bind me and loose them. Slay me and save them. All their ill be upon me. So, it is dear Jesus!'[3]

The love of Christ lit Samuel's face, it was as though his whole body was burning for Christ. Some thought he was so enthusiastic for preaching the Word of God that the excitement of it might make him fly out of the pulpit and go straight to heaven.

Thankfully he was also a man with his feet firmly on the ground. Sometimes he would burst into poetry, other times he would see the world as it was and use it skilfully as a teaching tool. Picture the day that Samuel

---

2. Thieves bands: this is another word Samuel used where we might use handcuffs or ropes instead.

3. From *The Loveliness of Christ*: Sermon xii, Banner of Truth

Samuel Rutherford

had the opportunity to observe some rather smart looking soldiers. They were dressed in their official uniforms and had a commanding presence with their medals and weaponry on show.

Samuel knew that several of the young men and women in his congregation would be very much impressed with the appearance of these men. He was glad that there were warriors like these willing to show courage to fight for their country, 'But,' he thought, 'I'm certainly glad that Anwoth doesn't require a garrison. Although, perhaps I need soldiers of a sort as I live out my life for God and His kingdom.'

'The first soldier that I need is ....' Samuel thought about this as he watched the smart uniforms march away 'Yes, it is – *The Fear of God*. Respect for God and His Word, fear that by my words or actions I would bring dishonour on Him – that is what I need as my first protection against sin.'

'Now, I suppose I would call my next soldier *Temperance*. But how do I explain that word to the young in my congregation? I could tell them that it means we must be in control of our desires and emotions. We're not to overdo the pleasures of the world. Because if we do, then we let the devil in and he is like a roaring lion going about seeking who he can devour.'[4]

The journey home to Anwoth brought with it the third, fourth and fifth soldiers.

---

4. 1 Peter 5:8

The Law, the Prince and the Scribe

'The third soldier, I will call him *Discretion*,' Samuel decided. 'That's another word for wisdom, particularly wise choices and decisions. When thoughts and ideas come into our hearts and minds, we need to consider where these thoughts have come from – are they from God or the devil?

'I can't really think of a good name for my fourth soldier,' Samuel pondered. 'I suppose I shall just have to give him a longer name than the others, *Suspicion of Our Own Ways*. The apostle Paul said to his young friend Timothy, 'In all things watch.'[5] We're to be careful because we can sin in everything that we do and say. Even in drinking a cup of water or eating a bite of bread. Nobody should think too well of himself because then he can too easily fall into sin. The Bible tells us that the heart is deceitful above all things and desperately wicked[6]. So, we need to be wary of what we want to do, even of the things we do every day. There is so much opportunity for us to disobey God.'

As Samuel walked past the holly bushes that stood by the manse and along by the honeysuckle, he thought of his fifth soldier. It was quite a sombre name, *Meditation on Death*. But in Samuel's life, where so many people perished from disease, death was never far away. It didn't matter if you were rich or poor sickness could take you no matter how many coins were in your pocket. In the few short years that Samuel had been

---

5. 2 Timothy 4:5.
6. Jeremiah 17:9

Samuel Rutherford

the minister of Anwoth, he had visited many people in their last days and even hours of life. Children too often perished from sudden, violent fevers. Death was a severe reality and it was unwise of people to ignore it. Across the whole country many people had died from plagues and epidemics. Sometimes whole families or several families in a community would be dead within weeks of each other. Samuel would urge his congregation, *'You must remember Christ and that death and judgment come in the night just like a thief. If you think about death and turn to Christ, then you will be blessed.'*

The sixth soldier came to Samuel's thoughts as he got ready for the supper that Eupham was preparing in the kitchen. The children were in bed and the maid had retired to her room for the night. It was just the two of them. A rare moment of peace and quiet. So Samuel took a few moments to try and come up with another name, but it was tricky. 'I'm just going to have to call him, *Practice Good and Walk with God*. Samuel knew that often the people of his parish were kept from their sleep by their worries and problems. But if they were absolutely honest with God, trusting in Him, living their lives always looking to God's mercy, justice, kindness and power, then their sleep would be sweet. Free from worry, their souls would be strong and protected from sin by a close walk with God.

The final seventh soldier came to Samuel as he got up from his prayers to climb into bed. 'Ah – we have the soldier of *Faith*,' Samuel rejoiced. 'The last of my valiant defenders. All seven of them now stand around my bed, protecting me in my sleep. God's soldiers in the service of Christ. They keep Christ in my soul and defend me.'

As he drifted off to sleep, he thought about writing these words down on some paper. These thoughts were worth keeping.

Letters, a Disguise and Tragedy

Those thoughts of Samuel's that were worth keeping would often find their way into sermons or letters. In fact, it is worth pointing out that in the future Samuel's Rutherford's letters were cherished perhaps as much as his sermons and the more learned publications. The letters certainly flew from Rutherford's pen thick and fast, or at least as fast as they could in the 1600s, when it was difficult to send post. Why was it difficult? Well, it was simply because you had to rely on your correspondence being taken to its destination by a man on horseback along a network of tracks and roads that were usually badly maintained and subject to poor weather. The 1600s was a time in history when a journey from one place to another might take several days, even weeks – and it was possible that you wouldn't get to your destination at all. There were dangers on the road when you lived in a century where there were conflicts and wars, disturbances, highway robbery and no police to call on.

However, a lot of Samuel's letters got to where they were meant to be. And many of his friends and contacts were thankful for that. He could not have known the future impact of his words — but the people who received his letters had more of an idea. Often his posts would arrive just at the right time, with just the right words they needed to hear. Some of these people were at the lowest points of their lives and in great distress, but the passionate heart of the pastor from Anwoth would draw alongside them even though he was days away on horseback.

One person he wrote to was Marion M'Naught. She had been amongst the very first visitors to the new minister and his family at Anwoth. She wasn't poor like many of the tenant farmers and came from quite a different background to some of the other people Samuel ministered to. Marion M'Naught was the wife of the Provost of Kirkcudbright. A provost was the Scottish equivalent of a Mayor. Over the years more than forty letters would make their way from Rutherford's pen to this godly woman.

Samuel was delighted to know her and said so in a letter to another friend, *'Blessed be the Lord that I have found in this country such a woman to whom Jesus is dearer than her own heart.'*

Marion had a young daughter called Grizzel. And it wasn't long after Samuel first met Mrs M'Naught that she suggested to him that Grizzel might be of use to him and his wife. 'She has a way with young children, and she is so full of energy. It would do her good to be in your family and I can see that she would be of great help to your young wife. You may not realise it, men don't always notice these things, but I think Eupham could do with some extra help around the house. She looked so tired the last time I saw her. I know that you and your wife are godly Christian people. Grizzel would learn a lot from you and I pray would turn in her heart to Christ under your guidance.'

Eupham and Samuel both saw the wisdom and benefits of this plan and before too long the two Rutherford children had a quick and energetic teenager running around after them.

Grizzel didn't really have much opportunity to miss her home or her mother as Kirkcudbright was not that far away and her mother loved to come to listen to Samuel Rutherford preach whenever the opportunity arose. She took lots of notes so that she could take these sermons home with her and think about them in the days that followed. One of the sermons she wrote down was from a communion service that Samuel was preaching. The Scripture verses he used were from the Song of Solomon. This was a book of the Bible that Samuel was strongly influenced by. He would often refer to Jesus Christ as being like a husband and the church like the bride – both descriptions are often used in that Old Testament book. Marion's notes show again how descriptive and poetic Samuel was when preaching the gospel, *'It is ordinary for man to beg from God, for we are His beggars; but it is a miracle to see God beg at man. Yet*

The Law, the Prince and the Scribe

here is the Potter begging from the clay;[1] the Saviour seeking from sinners! What is His request? All He asks is for just one sight of His bride. He is saying to her, 'My dear spouse, be kind to me, let me see your face ... tell me all your mind in prayer.'

Samuel was to spend much time and use a lot of ink and paper over the years writing to Marion and others like her. Grizzel was a great help to the weary young mother, giving Mrs Rutherford the energies she required to do other needful tasks in their growing household. For not only were there two children to add to the bodies in the manse, but there were other people who helped in the house and grounds as well. The manse would have had a live-in cook and maid. Households from that era often had what we would call servants living in the home or in a shelter above or alongside the barn. There was most likely a groomsman or someone to tend the garden. They all freed Samuel and his wife to do other things.

So, Eupham felt a responsibility for the people who shared their home and who worked alongside them. She knew that Samuel wouldn't be able to do all that he did without her help and that she couldn't do all that she did without their assistance. One way that she felt she could help her servants was to care for their souls while allowing her husband to get on with his sermon preparation. So, every Saturday evening she would gather the household together and do what her husband

---

1. God is described in the Bible as the Potter and human beings, his creation as clay. Read Isaiah 45:9, 64:8, Romans 9:21.

usually did – read the Scripture and ask them questions. Often the numbers in the household would be more than usual if there was a traveller who needed lodgings and a meal. People like this were readily welcomed to the manse and given a warm bed.

One evening a knock was heard at the manse door. The maid opened it to find a weary old man in a damp cloak and muddy boots. He was untidy to say the least and looked as if he had travelled a considerable distance. The maid knew that her mistress would want the visitor looked after. So, he was quickly shown to some warm, dry sleeping quarters. As she fed him a steaming bowl of stew in the kitchen, she was quick to explain to him the way things were done in the minister's house.

'It's the evening before the Lord's Day,' she explained smartly. 'So, the mistress will want us all to gather after you've had your meal. She will read God's Word to us and give us some questions from the minister's catechism. Have you heard of a catechism before?'

The old man nodded. The maid looked doubtful that such an untidy looking traveller would know any catechism questions far less the answers, so she explained to him what they were. 'Well it's a list of questions that have a list of answers. You learn the questions and the answers. These questions and answers are all about God and the Bible and what God requires of us and what the Lord Jesus has done for us. Don't worry if you don't know what to say. Nobody expects you to be a Bible scholar like the minister. Now, he's

The Law, the Prince and the Scribe

a man who knows his Scriptures!' The maid turned around to see to some of her final chores, a bit curious as to why the old gentleman had that funny twinkle in his eye. 'It's almost as though he is laughing at me secretly,' she thought.

That evening, before everyone went to bed, and as Samuel was in his study preparing the final passages of his sermon, Eupham gathered her family and household in the living room. There were chairs and a bench and a window seat. Everyone took their place and soon Eupham was reading God's Word and asking questions to which most of the listeners were able to answer in full. Not wanting their elderly guest to feel ignored or different to the others she thought of a question she could ask him. 'I'm sure he'll know the answer to this. Even my toddler knows how many commandments God has given us.' So, she asked the guest 'Can you tell me dear friend how many commandments there are?' The old man smiled and said, 'Eleven.'

Eupham just looked at him. She was astonished that there could be someone who knew so little about the Word of God. He didn't even know that there were ten commandments!

She politely pointed out his mistake and then when everyone was in their beds, she shared that evening's experience with Samuel. 'This stranger in our home must know virtually nothing of the Bible. He doesn't even know how many commandments there are. Here I was thinking I was giving him an easy question!'

Samuel Rutherford

Samuel agreed that it was an unusual question to get wrong and that it was sad to see people so ignorant of the things of God.

However, the following morning both Eupham and Samuel were to discover that things aren't always what they seem. Samuel, as was his custom, got up early and went for a walk – it was the one part of the day where he could be sure of being alone with God. He would go out of the house to a grove of trees and spend his time in prayer. But to his surprise, on that morning someone had arrived there before him. He wasn't alone. Underneath a pine tree, an elderly man was on his knees, deep in passionate prayer. 'This must be the stranger that Eupham told me about,' Samuel whispered to himself. Listening to the man praying, Samuel realised that here was a man who knew God and God's Word. When the prayer was over Samuel approached the traveller, curious to find out what his story was. Samuel saw the same twinkle in the eye that the maid had seen earlier and soon the story was out.

'My name is Archbishop Usher,' the traveller explained. 'And I have come here to listen to you preach, Samuel Rutherford. Forgive me for my secretiveness – in truth it is a little game of mine to disguise myself on occasion. I find that I get to the truth of the matter when people don't realise who I really am. As soon as they hear that I'm an 'Archbishop' well, they are all on their best behaviour bowing here and scraping there – and frankly I can't be bothered with it.

The Law, the Prince and the Scribe

I am on my way from England to my diocese in Armagh and found myself passing so near to Anwoth I thought I must go and hear that gentleman preach – the one I've been hearing so much about. I deliberately chose to dress in my shabbiest clothes and made sure that my boots were particularly dirty. In this way I could visit your parish while remaining totally anonymous. And by the way, that maid of yours did such a good job of cleaning those dirty boots that I must thank her kindly before I leave. However, I won't be leaving before I hear a sermon from your lips.'

To this Rutherford agreed. 'There's one condition though,' he said. 'I will preach a sermon if you agree to preach the other. We have two sermons on the Lord's Day in Anwoth.'

To this the archbishop readily agreed, and the men made their way back to the manse – one a Presbyterian, the other an Episcopalian – both eager to preach and both rejoicing at making a new friend.

That evening as Archbishop Usher preached, he cleared up a question that Mrs Rutherford had had about his knowledge of the Bible. He read from the Bible, John 13:34, 'A new commandment I give unto you, that ye love one another.'

'Ah!' Eupham thought. 'There's the eleventh commandment!'

The following day the old traveller, less shabby looking now and with very clean boots waved farewell to his hosts. Samuel smiled as he watched the

Samuel Rutherford

archbishop disappear over the horizon. It was so good to have friendship and fellowship with other Christians. And Archbishop Usher was such a godly man. It had been so good to listen to him pray. If only all Christians could live in such friendship. Usher was certainly someone who longed for Christians to love each other. Both Rutherford and Usher put their differences aside that day and focussed jointly on Jesus Christ.

It had been a beautiful experience of friendship and joy, but that day was one of the last days of peace in the Rutherford home for quite some time. It wasn't long before the bustling manse became quite a different place altogether.

'Have you heard the news,' hushed voices spoke in urgent tones as one after another passed on the news from the manse. Sickness was visiting the manse. The congregation was very concerned for the poor family, but for fear of spreading the illness further, people deliberately stayed away.

Where it started and what exactly it was is difficult to say.

For weeks now there had been no sound of baby gurgles in the kitchen, no toddler running around squealing about some find or other in the garden. Grizzel's fascination with saving up for a new dress was put to one side as both of her charges sank into a listless inactivity and then a violent fever. There were no 'wee[2] bairns' playing by the stream. All was silent.

---

2. Wee – broad scots word for little.

The Law, the Prince and the Scribe

Soon it was as silent as the grave for both Rutherford children perished in quick succession. To make matters worse, at the same time Eupham came down with a sickness that caused her great physical and mental pain. Her condition didn't kill her, at least not at first, for it lasted many months.

The young mother who had lost both her infants lay at death's door herself. Samuel wasn't in the peak of health either, but he gathered what energy he could to spend hours earnestly praying for her recovery. A doctor had been sent for, but there was nothing he could do. Eupham's illness was a powerful one and it had a deep hold on her body and her mind. The pain was intense. One morning, as the songbird sang as usual in the honeysuckle and the sun rose over the bell tower of the Anwoth Kirk, Eupham breathed her last and Samuel found himself alone, the last surviving member of his little Anwoth family.

It was a time of great personal suffering. Physically, emotionally, and spiritually exhausted, Samuel barely knew what to do with himself. He had never felt so weary and alone, yet even in this dark trial he knew that Jesus was with him. The words he wrote in a letter prove that Samuel accepted this tragedy as being part of God's plan. *'The Lord has done it. Blessed be His name.'*

And knowing that God was in control meant that when others faced the same heartache, Samuel knew where to send them.

Samuel Rutherford

When a woman in his congregation lost her husband through death, Samuel reminded her that her '*Lord Jesus Christ would have compassion on a sad-hearted servant.*' ³

In later years when Samuel had suffered even more trials and difficulties, he was still able to bring comfort to others through his pen. Because he had been given by God that great grief of losing a child, he could draw alongside grieving parents in a way that others could not. Samuel had the gift of empathy – when someone can understand how another is feeling. His own suffering meant that he could empathise with those who had lost a loved one. He knew how they felt and how to help them. His talent for words meant he said what was needed to be said and he could turn those sorrowing hearts to Christ.

In one letter the grieving Anwoth scribe wrote to a mother who had lost a young daughter, '*You have lost a child; no, she is not lost to you who is found in Christ. She is not sent away but only sent before. She is like a star that has gone out of your sight. That star is not dead but shines in another hemisphere. You don't see your daughter, yet she shines in another country. . . . Prepare yourself; you are nearer your child this day than you were yesterday. While you spend your time in mourning for her, you are speedily following after her. I pray that the Comforter may bind up your wounds and that His grace may be with you more and more abundantly.*'

To other parents he offered the following advice, '*Let your children be as flowers borrowed from God. If the flowers*

---

3. Taken from Samuel Rutherford's letter CV dated 1637

die or wither thank God for a summer loan of them and keep on the most intimate terms with Him.'

To anyone who was going through hardship and difficulty he urged them to *'Think about what Jesus Christ is doing in this.'*

And one of the things Christ did in the middle of Samuel's sufferings was bring a young teenage girl to repentance. Sending Grizzel home to her mother Samuel was glad to write to Marion M'Naught that her daughter was now more keen to get a Bible of her own than a new dress. However, he suggested to her mother that it might be a good idea to give her both. And here again is a gentle reminder that even in his own sufferings, Samuel's thoughts often focussed on the needs and wishes of others.

The sufferings that Samuel went through during this period of his life were what you would call terrible. You could say it was impossible to go through anything worse. But just because that point in his life was the most heartbreaking, it didn't mean that Samuel's sufferings were at an end.

Archbishop Usher would have liked the Episcopalians and the Presbyterians to exist together. However, there were a lot of other people who were not willing for people like Samuel to gain any more influence than they already had. Bishop Thomas Sydserf, the Bishop of Galloway, was an arrogant individual. Sydserf looked on men like Samuel with an intense jealousy of their achievements and a strong dislike of their principles.

But Samuel and others like him were more concerned about following their conscience than the demands and threats of men. The fact was though that men like Sydserf got their power from the Crown – and in the 1600s the Crown had all the say.

Real Friends and Real Enemies

There were, as usual, several letters on Samuel's desk. He could see the way the world was going. Men like Bishop Sydserf were flexing their muscles, making sure people knew that they were in charge of the church. Sydserf had made it plain that he was not for Samuel Rutherford gaining more influence in the area. He had put his foot down when the people from Kirkcudbright had suggested that Samuel would be their choice of next minister. Sydserf was not going to allow Rutherford, a known Presbyterian, become the minister there – it was a bigger and more influential town than Anwoth. 'It's better he sticks to a little-known country backwoods pastorate. If someone like Rutherford is let loose in a more well-appointed parish who knows what he'll get up to,' Sydserf grumbled. So, Samuel didn't leave for pastures new – but that suited him fine. He didn't want to leave his flock in Anwoth. It was, in his opinion, the fairest place in all of Scotland and he would never choose to leave it.

The Law, the Prince and the Scribe

There were other reasons why it was good for Samuel to stay where he was. Anwoth was in quite a prominent position despite it being off the beaten track and sparsely populated. It was what you would call strategically important because it was on a highway that led directly from England to Ireland. It was also right in the heart of south-west Scotland, an area well-known for Presbyterianism. In addition to that, the area had a very influential nobleman named Lord Gordon. He was a keen supporter of Samuel, but in this troublesome and turbulent time it seemed as though you couldn't really rely on anybody, even your friends.

The year 1636 was going to be one of those years when Samuel Rutherford learned who his real friends were. They certainly weren't the bishops, the king or Lord Gordon. All these people either plotted against him, attacked him or abandoned him.

Samuel had made it clear that he was against what was happening to the church in Scotland. He wrote a book[1] that really angered the Scottish bishops including Sydserf. Many of the bishops supported the idea that salvation was not simply a gift from God – you had to work to be forgiven of your sins. Rutherford disagreed. '*Salvation is a free gift from God,*' he declared. '*Grace, grace, free grace. All the blessings of salvation, all the good qualities and virtues of Christ were given by God without us giving*

---

1. Rutherford published thirteen major theological treatises in his lifetime, amounting to just over 7,000 pages of text. There were also other works, including sermons, letters, a catechism with 562 questions and answers as well as a variety of political writings.

Samuel Rutherford

anything in return.' Rutherford's book was published in Amsterdam in 1636 – after which Sydserf demanded that Samuel renounce Presbyterian worship and government. Samuel Rutherford refused.

He wrote a letter to Lord Kenmure's wife who was far more sympathetic to Rutherford's cause than her husband. *'The bishop wants us to swallow our light and vomit our conscience by giving into these demands.'* Samuel would not. Lord Kenmure already had. He had been given lands and titles by the king and when he had an opportunity to take a stand for the Presbyterian cause, he buckled. Instead of taking his place in Parliament and saying what he really thought, he pretended to be sick and disappeared to his estates in the country.

Things got even worse when some of Samuel's personal papers fell into the wrong hands. The Bishop of Galloway read them and was furious at how Samuel described the leadership of the Church of Scotland as corrupt. When Samuel heard that these papers had actually been laid before the king, he was anxious, even scared, but he understood that the power of God was the power not only in the land, but the world. There was a King of kings – his Lord Jesus Christ.

'I hang by a thread,' Rutherford wrote to one of his friends. *'But it is a thread of Christ's spinning.'*

By the time spring came, Samuel had been summoned by Sydserf to attend the court at Wigton. It was there that Samuel was banished from Anwoth, no longer allowed to preach to his congregation. But

The Law, the Prince and the Scribe

Sydserf hoped to punish him even more. That would need a higher court. So, Samuel was instructed to appear before the Court of High Commission in Edinburgh.

It was a summer morning when Samuel finally turned his back on Anwoth. Closing the door behind him, he took one last breath savouring the aroma of pine needle and honey suckle. The songbird still sang, the roses still bloomed but as he walked down the path a bird's egg lay crushed on the grass. 'In pieces,' he muttered as he left his home. He hoped that his ministry would not be as broken and useless as that shattered shell.

However, as he began to walk along the track, the same one that nine years before he had ridden on through a storm, he could see this man and that woman, a child, a youth, an old grandmother, all lining the road to wish him well. A few of the younger and fitter of the congregation walked with him. 'We'll not leave you as you have not left us.' And they accompanied him, over 100 miles, all the way to Edinburgh.

The case took three days of intense questioning. Samuel simply refused to conform to their commands. The court insisted he adopt the method of worship that the king demanded. Samuel said no. He refused to call the bishops 'Lord' which really riled them. There were a few voices that tried to defend him but, in the end, Rutherford was forbidden to preach anywhere in Scotland. And to ensure that he was removed from all who loved and supported him he was banished to the most northerly city in the country – the city of Aberdeen. A place well known for its support of Episcopacy.

'He'll not get up to anything there,' one of the bishops sneered. 'There will be few to sympathise with him in that place.'

When the sentence was announced Samuel turned to a companion.

'There is nothing more honourable than to suffer for the truth. This honour my kind Lord has bestowed on me. I am to suffer for my princely King Jesus. I am going to my King's palace in Aberdeen. Tongue, pen and wit cannot express my joy.'

Samuel wasn't even allowed to return home to Anwoth to collect his possessions. He had to leave immediately for Aberdeen. That was a journey of over 200 miles. Undaunted, his Anwoth friends went with him, determined to see their beloved pastor safely to his destination. After many days of hard walking, strange beds in noisy inns and difficult weather, Samuel, and his sorry companions eventually arrived at the city of Aberdeen. Essentially Rutherford was going to be under house arrest although it wasn't a prison. He would have some freedom to go about, but other than that he was stuck. He could not leave. A small rented room in Upperkirkgate Street in the centre of town was where he laid his head. What a sad figure he must have looked, a lonely man, in a sombre room, with no one to talk to.

The Law, the Prince and the Scribe

Though, it wasn't the absence of friends and familiar faces that hit him the hardest. It wasn't the fact that he was in a city that appeared to him to be very unfriendly. The sorest part of his punishment were the orders that on no account was he to preach at all! The bishops of the town were willing at first to let him debate with them on certain issues, but then Rutherford's intelligence and wit got the better of them. After the third discussion they decided that debating with Rutherford was not good for their egos. It didn't do for the 'banished minister' to show them up in this way.

So, not only was Samuel banned from preaching, the bishops didn't even want to hear him discuss or debate. It really was too much! Samuel Rutherford complained that his one joy next to Christ was to preach. *'My dumb Sabbaths[2] burden my heart. They are like a stone tied to a bird's foot. I think the sparrows and swallows that build their nests at Anwoth are blessed birds indeed'*.

Samuel's heart broke for his congregation when news of their sorrow and difficulties made its way to his northern prison.

They were without a pastor, without *their* pastor, and they felt that keenly. Samuel did too. And although he couldn't preach with his lips he could with his pen. For many months his letters slowly made their way 200 miles back down to the lowlands, encouraging his old congregation, as well as friends and loved ones –

---

2. Sabbath: This is another word for Sunday or the Lord's day. Samuel longed to preach on the Lord's day instead of being silent.

encouraging them to turn to Christ, to follow Christ, to trust in God.

Taking up his pen and paper in the little draughty, friendless room he would write his letters in sorrow but fighting to retain some of his old joy.

'I write to you from Aberdeen where I am a prisoner by order of the authorities. They have judged that I have uttered treason against the king. And for that reason, they have banished me from you and condemned me to silence.

My closed mouth, my silent Sabbaths, the memory of my communion with Christ in many fair, fair days in Anwoth have almost broken my faith in half. I had one joy next to Jesus my Lord and that was to preach Him to this faithless generation. And that has been taken from me.

My sorrow makes me think that Christ is angry with me. But I wish to give no credit to my sorrow when it suggests hard thoughts of Christ. Yet these thoughts awake with me in the morning. What can I do? I am like a dry tree. I can't plant. I can't water. If only I had three shepherds that I could speak to about my Lord Jesus. I would be satisfied to be the poorest pastor in the land.

My other worry is 'What have I done in Anwoth?' Is the work that God began there like a bird dying in its shell? On the last day when I stand before Christ will I have anything to show for my work there?

But I pray to Christ to pardon my whining unbelieving sadness and sorrow. I am sorry that I even thought that Christ was angry with me. For truly I am a debtor to His love. I wish He would help me to do without His comforts and to give thanks and believe even when the sun is not shining. I have no strength of my own to carry me to heaven; I must go there borrowing my strength from Jesus.

I must say that it has been good for me to come to Aberdeen, to learn new things about Christ. I have learned to believe His promises even when it appears otherwise. It is true that often I am blown back with a storm of doubting; yet truly even when I am imprisoned there is the perfume of the deep love of Christ. I creep under my Lord's wing in the great storm and the water can not reach me. We may sing even in a winter storm, as we may expect the summer sun at the end of the year.

No created power in hell or out of hell can spoil our song of joy. In that hope we rest. Beloved, stand fast in the truth of Christ which you have received. Ride out the storm. Christ is your firm anchor. We expect trouble here. We are God's wheat and we must go through Satan's sieve, but our souls shall not faint, neither shall our faith fail in the day of trial. Please pray for me, God's prisoner, that He would send me again among you to preach and minister to your needs.

Grace be with you.'

Some of his letters to Anwoth were less depressed and you could still hear something of the voice of the concerned pastor.

Memories of Anwoth would bring him to write to his congregation, urging them to flee from sin. *'Sin is at our right hand hindering us to hear, pray, believe, hope. It is like the wind in the face of a weak traveller that blows him some steps back where he goes one forward. This sin is like an ivy plant that goes about a tree, wrapping about us in every way. It is like a serpent that bites our heel. Sin is like a mocker, it promises us much but gives us the wind. And yet we believe it? How can we shake off this sin that dwells in us and goes around us, even to the grave?'*

Samuel urged the people of Anwoth to turn to Christ. It was only Christ's power that could break the strangle hold of sin. *'As we repent and advance in holiness, we conquer this indwelling sin.'*

Remembering the seven soldiers he had imagined all those months ago in the lowlands he quickly noted down the names and shared them with his congregation, *'The Fear of God,' 'Temperance' 'Discretion' 'Suspicion of Our Own ways' 'Meditation on Death' 'Practice Good and Walk with God' and finally 'Faith'.*

'These are the graces of God that keep Christ in the soul.'

As Samuel struggled with the bitter blasts that came off the North Sea, he wondered how he could ever have thought that the weather in Anwoth was cold. It was positively balmy warm in comparison. In the middle of winter, a walk down the centre of Aberdeen was like turning your face into a barrage of icy needles. Icicles hung from the eaves like balancing javelins. The wind could only be described as cutting. Everything was cold, even the people. Samuel regarded the locals as giving a *'dry kindness'* if any at all. But Samuel did his best not to let the situation crush him and time and time again he reminded himself that he was *'The Lord's prisoner.'*

There was one other way that Samuel kept his spirit's up – his time in Aberdeen was a rich time for writing books, and after a few months he found that nobody seemed to be that bothered if he went visiting. When he found the time to socialise, he discovered that the conversation often turned towards spiritual things, so Samuel would make sure that he turned the conversation to Christ. He may not have been preaching in a pulpit, but he was preaching in a parlour. And he was finally making some friends!

One of the letters he wrote from the city shared some interesting and encouraging news. And as he wrote he had just a little smirk on his face.

'There are some blossomings of Christ's kingdom in this town. And the ministers are raging! But I like a rumbling and roaring devil best.'[3]

As he sent another letter off into the wide and turbulent world of 1600s Scotland, he found himself thinking that perhaps there was a reason for his banishment to this freezing city.

'Even if they do what they are threatening to do and banish me to Caithness or Orkney – they can never banish me from Jesus.'

In that he was confident.

---

3. Taken from one of Samuel Rutherford's letters dated 1637 Letter: CCXLIII

Events Belong to God

A phrase that you may be familiar with is 'the darkest hour comes just before the dawn.' When someone says that it means that just when things seem to be at their most hopeless, the situation changes for the better. And certainly, the church in Scotland was in a very dark place indeed. People like Rutherford couldn't even imagine how things could possibly turn around, but they prayed that it would. And God was listening to their prayers!

Samuel tried to think of ways to encourage the persecuted believers that he corresponded with.

Again, it involved him looking for examples from day to day life.

When the bitter winter was over, Samuel started to go on walks again. They weren't long, but there was one walk that took him by a small loch. Several young lads were larking about there as young lads do. Samuel smiled, 'The shepherd boys in Anwoth would play the same game,' as he saw one boy after another jump into the loch and then try to hold a companion down under the surface. A lot of yelling and splashing was involved.

The Law, the Prince and the Scribe

On occasion Samuel thought the antics got a bit rough, but he could see that all the boys were good swimmers. And although a lad would do his best to keep another one down, he never really succeeded for long.

'That's just like the church of Christ today,' Samuel realised. 'We're struggling as wicked men try to keep us down. The levels of persecution, according to my dear flock in Anwoth, are getting worse by the day. *But our cause remains under the water only as long as wicked men hold us there. Their arm will eventually get weary. And then the just cause shall swim above.*'

Turning to walk back towards the city once more Samuel made his way by a barnyard only to be 'greeted' by a rather unfriendly sheep dog. As is often the case the dog's bark was worse than its bite – and its growls and snarls were quickly rebuked by its master who said, 'Away with ye Jock. Dinna bother the gent.' And to Samuel he called out, 'Never mind the beast. He only barks at strangers. And his teeth are that crooked he could dae ye nae damage at all.'

Samuel waved and went on his way, remembering how he had told his congregation in Anwoth in happier times, *'If you were not strangers here the dogs of this world would not bark at you. The world is one of the enemies that we must fight with. But it is a vanquished and defeated enemy, a beaten soldier. Christ, our Captain, has said, "Be of good courage for I have overcome the world."'* [1]

Open your hearts to the Spirit of love for love "beareth all things, believeth all things, hopeth all things, endureth all

---

1. John 16:33.

things."[2] Love has strong broad shoulders. High mountains and heavy burdens will not tire love. Love will never sweat, faint or fall in a swoon for God helps love. Get love and no burden that Christ lays on you will be heavy. Pray for your enemies. Remember how many sins Christ has forgiven you for. So, you should forgive also. May the Lord Jesus lead you to see the beauty of His way of forgiveness, mercy and loving kindness.'[3]

Samuel hurried on down the hill, the sound of the dog echoing behind him. The dogs of the world had barked at him and his congregation in the past. They were still doing so. But his beautiful Lord Jesus had those dogs on a strong leash.

Sometimes Samuel still struggled with what he called 'ups and downs'. He felt as though he was set adrift in the ocean where the swell caught him and his feet could not touch the ground. Then a prayer or a passage of Scripture would soothe his heart. His unsteady feet found a grip on the foundation of Jesus Christ. He was his strength.

In his darkest moments Samuel found himself angry and impatient with God. He felt as though he was a withered root that had been dug up by a farmer and cast out like rubbish. Samuel even suspected that God had no use for him. 'When will this be over?' he cried in anguish. 'What's wrong, Lord?' Samuel pleaded. 'Why have you thrown me away like this? I only wanted to be a faithful preacher for you?' Samuel just couldn't understand.

---

2. 1 Corinthians 13:7.

3. Taken from Letter LIV to Marion M'Naught. Likely written before Rutherford's exile to Aberdeen.

But then God would open Samuel's eyes to the truth which was – no matter what happened, or didn't happen, *'Duties are ours. Events are God's.'*

God was always in charge.

Samuel would think of the large ships crashing through the waves of the North Sea. Some could be seen far on the horizon making their way to the harbour – firm in their course, a strong captain at the helm. Samuel realised that despite everything, his life was the same. Christ was his captain, steering his life, steering the world. And there was nobody better to have behind the steering wheel than Jesus. Another picture that came to Samuel's mind, when seeing a vessel rising and falling with the waves, was how each of these ships had a compass. He imagined the ship's captain earnestly studying the compass as he made his way into some port or other. And with that picture he wrote the following advice to another Christian, *'Your heart is not the compass that Christ steers by.'*

Samuel realised that because people so often saw their own longings and desires as being most important, they felt that surely their longings and desires were of primary importance to God. It simply was not the case. God's plans were not man's plans. His thoughts not our thoughts.

Samuel realised that he had to preach that message to himself. He couldn't understand why God had let him suffer all these problems – but God did know what was best.

Samuel Rutherford

'*What further trials are before me I know not,*' Samuel acknowledged. '*But I know that Christ has saved me and that I will one day be in heaven beyond men's wrongs. Beloved in Christ, thoughts of your souls depart not from me even in my sleep. Until it please God that I see you and be permitted to minister to you, you have the prayers of a prisoner of Christ.*'

When Samuel received letters, it seemed as though they often contained bad news. There were always tidings of one or another minister who was banished. George, Samuel's brother, had been arrested and removed from his post as teacher at Kirkcudbright. It wasn't enough to banish Samuel Rutherford, even those people who loved and supported him were being sought out for punishment. In Aberdeen the ministers were even preaching against Samuel and his beliefs. They couldn't care less that Samuel was sitting in the congregation listening to them!

Thankfully, some of the people who had become Samuel's close friends in the city wrote letters asking for the banished pastor to be freed. These letters didn't have any impact, but Samuel began to appreciate what true friendship really was. There were friends and family who were willing to lose their lives and their livelihoods by supporting him. That was a comfort. But there still were others who didn't have the courage to stand up for the Lord.

The city of Aberdeen was a tough school for Samuel – but it was a valuable one.

In a letter to Lady Kenmure, Samuel admitted that he had learned more in his six months of prison in

Aberdeen than he had learned in nine years of ministry in Anwoth.

Samuel knew that all his troubles came *'through Christ's fingers.'* And that God was king over all his circumstances.

However, one of Samuel's greatest regrets was seeing how quickly the national church had gone downhill and how easy it was for men of power to sit back and do nothing. He warned anyone who would listen that, *'You are not worthy of Jesus if you will not take a blow for the Master's sake'*

The believers in Scotland began to wonder if the struggle would ever end. Would they ever be free? Well, one day the king just went too far, over stretching his powers in the nation of Scotland. There had been many who had been willing to compromise, who had just said, 'Let the king have his way.' But when the king had his way too often Scotland decided that she had had enough!

Like a bully, King Charles had paid no regard for what the people of the land wanted or the church. Bishops had been forced on the church by his father, so he followed that example by forcing a book of law on the Church of Scotland, along with a liturgy and book of common prayer. These included many phrases taken from Roman Catholicism. This all happened in 1637, a year after Rutherford had been banished to Aberdeen. Rutherford, who was kept informed about all the national events, was infuriated at the demands of the king on the kirk. And across the nation many men and women refused to accept 'Laud's Liturgy' as it came to be called. It appeared as though the tide might be beginning to turn.

On Sunday, 23rd July in 1637 the book of Common Prayer was used for the first time in St. Giles Cathedral – or at least they tried to use it. One woman, a market trader called Jenny Geddes, was so incensed at the idea she yelled in broad scots, 'Dar ye say mass[4] in ma lug!' And promptly threw her wooden stool at the preacher's head. Soon the whole church was in turmoil with loud cries of protest. When this all spilled out onto the street a riot began. The entire city was fired up and then it just spread and spread across the nation. Still the king would not compromise. Anyone who stood against him would be declared a rebel. 'I would rather die than yield to their impertinent demands!' he bellowed.

This forced the Church of Scotland to take matters into their own hands. In February 1638 over 1000 Scottish ministers and other leaders gathered at Greyfriars Kirk in Edinburgh to sign 'The National Covenant.' It was a powerful experience for many of the men who signed their names - some even signed it in their own blood. The king would no longer control the church. In this covenant they set out the beliefs that they stood for and those that they stood against.

---

4. Mass: This is the Roman Catholic method of remembering the death of Christ. The Roman Catholics believe that the bread and wine become the physical body and blood of Christ. The Protestant/Reformed church believe that the bread and wine are symbols or pictures of the body and blood – reminders to us of how Jesus died on the cross to save us from our sins.

The Law, the Prince and the Scribe

It wasn't a statement against the king. They were clear on that. This wasn't a revolution. But they were adamant that nobody was going to force the church to do anything against her will ever again. And that was when the Covenanters began.

Samuel wasn't there at the signing of the covenant, but as soon as he heard about it, he packed his bags and left the city. The flame had been lit. The nation had turned, and Samuel knew he could leave without asking permission from anyone. He was free once more.

With quick stop at Edinburgh he broke his silence by preaching – how good that must have felt after so long! Then he went where his heart was longing to be – back to Anwoth.

As he reached the top of the last hill, the view opened beneath him showing him the pine trees and the church tower, the trail of chimney smoke from the already lit fireplace at the manse. Samuel's joy was written all over his face. In the distance a young shepherd lad whooped and hollered. 'The pastor's back. Rutherford's hame[5] at last!'

And then something happened to Samuel, one of the unusual things that happens when someone is truly happy. A tear trickled down his face, even though his heart was singing. 'I'm never going to leave this place ever again. Not if I can help it.'

But that's one thing you should never do – you should never say never. Not when God has plans.

---

5. Hame: The Scottish pronunciation of home.

The King who Huffed and Puffed

Although the king had not got his way in Scotland, he was still powerful enough and angry enough to cause problems. He huffed and puffed from his London palaces, but then he realised that it's better to know what your enemy is up to than live in ignorance. The Church of Scotland wanted to call a General Assembly (a special meeting for making church decisions.) They would do this with or without Charles I's permission, so Charles decided to grant his permission anyway and send a delegate to keep an eye on things.

Rutherford was one of the delegates who attended the assembly. He left Anwoth with a spring in his step. It was different this time. As he walked briskly down the manse garden, he was leaving knowing that he was coming back and the fact that the Assembly was meeting again was a great encouragement to him.

'What a change in such a short time,' he exclaimed. 'The depression and dark days of my Aberdeen imprisonment seem like a distant memory now.' There was still antagonism against the Presbyterians and Covenanters, but at least the people could make decisions in the church without having to buckle under the king's demands or whims.

Of course, the king's delegate had to cause problems and he tried to. However, the Assembly had a new strength and paid no attention to his blustering and intimidations. 'The church has a right to assemble and this is a right from God that the king cannot take away.'

Several key pieces of business were attended to. Committees were appointed to oversee tasks and issues. The Book of Common Prayer was removed as were the bishops. But it wasn't just things from their troubled past that the church was sorting out, they were also looking to the future.

'We need to train up the next generation of preachers. And the best way to do this is to put men of talent in key positions. We need to reinvigorate the universities with ministers of faith, excellent scholars.'

Samuel nodded in agreement as he listened to the discussion. It was so good to be here where these decisions were being made – planning for the future, the future of God's church. But then he was astonished – someone had said his name. Had he misheard? No, he hadn't!

One of the other delegates had gone on to say that because of his excellent writings it was clear that Samuel Rutherford was just the calibre of scholar they were looking for. 'He's also an ardent supporter of the cause and the covenants,' someone added. 'The ideal man for the post.'

Samuel found his lips dry and his heart in his mouth. He muttered and stuttered as the discussion moved on.

'I move that Samuel Rutherford be placed in the vacant chair of theology at St. Mary's college at St. Andrew's University,' another delegate announced.

Several men nodded their heads and voiced their agreement.

Samuel unsteadily stood up to add his voice to the discussion. But his initial protest was brushed away. Samuel returned to Anwoth – resorting to letter-writing to get his view across.

Before he set out his protest in paper, he decided to make a list of his points. 'That way I'll make a clear argument for my cause.'

It is not right to remove a minister and bring sorrow to his congregation.

I don't have the gifts or the mind for this task.

Removing a minister without the congregation's consent must be unlawful.

I sometimes even feel unable for the task here in Anwoth, so why should they give me an even harder one?

I should also get the congregation to write letters.

And that's what they did. The people of Anwoth sent a petition begging that they be allowed to keep their beloved pastor. Being deprived of Rutherford they exclaimed, would bring them 'bitter grief.'

In addition to the congregation, many noblemen and ministers from across the region of Galloway also wrote in protest. They pointed out that Samuel's work had been greatly blessed in their community and that Samuel's own health was not that robust. They believed that the stress of leaving Anwoth and taking on the responsibilities in St. Andrew's could weaken his tired-out body even further.

However, all their protests and Samuel's were pushed to one side. Samuel eventually realised that he had to give in. There was one condition though. And only if the Assembly agreed to that condition would he reluctantly leave for St. Andrews.

'Those months I spent in Aberdeen were a trial for one reason – my silence. I will only go to St. Andrews if I'm allowed to preach.'

The church authorities were more than happy to grant him this request. And when Samuel left his beloved congregation behind in Anwoth he went to St. Andrews with the promise that he could be an associate minister alongside another pastor.

It would make the final decision something he could cope with, but it still broke his heart to leave behind his congregation, the people he had been separated from so cruelly and then at last reunited with.

He arrived at St. Andrews, a city on the east coast of Scotland that had strong Reformation links. However, the city had forgotten its heritage and now had little evidence of good biblical preaching or teaching. In fact, the city was well known for its religious superstitions. Samuel had his work cut out for him. As a teacher of young men, he once again witnessed how easy it was for them to make shipwreck of their souls.

He would grasp hold of any opportunity in the lecture theatre, tutorial or the pulpit to warn young men about the dangers of a Christless life.

'What a nest of dangerous temptations youth is — the devil finds in you at this age a swept chamber and a garnished lodging for himself.

Give now in the morning of your life I pray you, your mind, your will, your heart to Christ. Happy is your soul if Christ enter and take the keys of the house let Him command all your deeds and thoughts, plans and desires.

I entreat you, while yet your years are few, climb the mountain of God. Hold fast to Christ. Hear His voice only. The gospel is God's candle to let you see the way to heaven; study it with diligence. Love not the world nor the things of this world. Give God some of your thoughts both morning and evening and forget Him not at any time.

I pray young men, that there are some among you who will fear God and give your souls and bodies completely to His service. Oh, what a sweet couple are youth and grace, Christ and a young man!'

Rutherford's personal example and his conscientious teaching of Systematic Theology, Church History and Hebrew soon began to have an effect. What had been a lacklustre university, where students were more likely to be conversant in profanity than in any actual studies, now became a true source of godly men, intent on becoming preachers of the Word.

The Law, the Prince and the Scribe

At the same time, King Charles started to huff and puff once more. The Scots were thorns in his side, and he wanted to scratch at them – to remove them from his skin completely. He was arrogant enough to think that he could squash the Covenanters. Arrogance is a dangerous vice in a king. Charles I decided to invade Scotland. Did he consider the strength of a well-trained and well-commanded army? Did he think about how the Scottish Lords could muster 20,000 men loyal to the cause? Did he pay attention to the fact that the opposing forces had officers who had experience in battle and the respect of their men? Did he realise that because he had banished his own parliament, he had no money to train his own troops, far less win a war? No, he did not.

Charles I showed his vanity and his stupidity – unfortunately both these traits would eventually lead to his death.

To start with, Charles and his troops were sent packing. Fortress after fortress was overturned by the Covenanter army. Each lord had his own colours flying above his troops. The new covenanting motto emblazoned on each one, 'For Christ's Crown and Covenant.'

The Covenanters gave Charles ample opportunity to suffer defeat gracefully. They wrote to him declaring their loyalty to the Crown as long as he let them alone and recognised that the church was independent to the Crown.

Samuel Rutherford

A treaty was signed, and Charles made promise after promise — none of which he kept. He never had any plans to. He was just biding his time for a better opportunity to come his way. He hoped that at some point in the future the situation would change so that he could disregard any of the promises he had made. It seems as though Charles was not someone who learned a lesson very well. In 1640 when Charles I didn't get his way again, he sent in his army – again! The Covenanters won again! But this time the Covenanters invaded England and captured Newcastle.

Charles I faced another humiliating defeat. And here we see one of the strange things about arrogant men, that even when they are humiliated, they still think they're the best. Charles decided that he should recall his parliament — the men he had disposed of when he thought he had no need of them. Now he wanted them back. He had no money or resources to call on and he had promised to pay the Scots their expenses for the war. Parliament would have to give him the money — he certainly didn't have it — let them raise taxes or something, Charles blustered.

He didn't realise that it wasn't going to be as easy as all that. Parliament was no pushover and in fact a lot of the men that Charles had kicked out of power were actually supporters of the Covenanters. They were called Puritans. They looked north of the border and liked what they saw. The church there now had freedom and independence. The Puritans wanted the same in the south. Charles was not going to get his own way by just calling Parliament back and telling these men what to do. It seemed that the king who thought he was the best, had enemies on both sides of the border.

Do you remember what we were saying about the 1600s being a turbulent time? It certainly was.

It's good to see though that nice things happen during turbulent times – ordinary things happen during conflicts and battles. And during this time when a king was huffing and puffing, and fortresses were falling and treaties being made – Samuel Rutherford had caught the eye of a young woman, Jean McMath, and she had caught his eye and there was a marriage. For a second time Samuel was in love and children were on the way. And it wasn't just children that would bring change to Rutherford and his home.

The nation from the north to the south was in turmoil for one reason or another. A civil war had started, and Episcopacy no longer enjoyed the position of power that it once had. Because of that, new plans and projects were afoot. Samuel and his family would be at the very centre of them!

Look at Scotland!

The Puritans in Parliament were not just going to sit back and let the king have it all his own way. They took charge and made decisions, one of which was setting up a Grand Committee on religion. This was to meet every week in order to discuss how to reform the church.

'Look at Scotland,' people often said. 'They've done it and done it well. We should at least try to do something similar.'

There was some concern that the king would react against this move for change. There certainly was a long list of complaints. There were doctrines and policies that the church now wanted to abandon. And then again some that they wanted to restore.

The king decided to go along with things for now and even made the suggestion that Parliament should set up an assembly or some such meeting to discuss things. Perhaps he felt that a meeting of this sort would delay the matter, bogging decisions down in a mass of debate. However, he couldn't have been more wrong. Members of Parliament thought it was a great idea so they started to plan it out. 'Let's gather godly and learned men from across the nation to discuss the whole matter. We will get their expertise in spiritual matters – men from all the different sides of the church.'

There was actually great enthusiasm for the king's idea. That was when Charles realised that perhaps his suggestion would cause him problems so he changed his tune and tried to thwart the assembly at every opportunity. However, now that the ball had started to roll there was no stopping it. Even without the king's consent the Westminster Assembly was started.

An ordinance[1] was finally issued by both houses of Parliament on 12th June 1643. It declared that the present church government was evil and a great impediment to reformation and the growth of religion. The church needed to be cleared of all false slander and lies. And its government should be agreeable to God's holy Word.

A list of men were called to attend the assembly. There were 151 men in total and they came from all the different branches of the Christian church. There were 121 ministers and within that number there were four bishops as well as Presbyterians and Independents. There were also commoners, so that a wide range of opinions would be expressed and not just those thoughts of the high-up and well-educated. The decision was made that the assembly should also approach the Church of Scotland to gain assistance from their experience.

---

1. Ordinance: An authoritative command or order

Samuel Rutherford

Which was why, after the assembly had started on the first day of July, a group of five delegates from Scotland began their travels by ship down the east coast to London. Samuel Rutherford was one of them, and his wife Jean was with him.

One little infant accompanied them, but they had left the buried bodies of two other children behind in St. Andrews. Yet again, tragedy and illness had struck the Rutherford home, and it would not be the last.

Despite heartache, Samuel was willing to answer the call to assist at this great assembly. The journey would be no easy task. He knew that – but this was the right thing to do.

When he and Jean and the bairn arrived at the harbour with their belongings, Samuel did his best to encourage his wife who was anxious at the thought of the difficult journey ahead.

'I hope the little one won't be sick,' she said anxiously.

Samuel gently held his wife by the shoulder. 'The child will get used to it soon enough and look at the ship we will be sailing in. It's a strong vessel, just the one to go to sea in.'

'But what about the storms?' his wife sighed. 'This time of year is notorious for bad weather. And then there might be whales or pirates or...'

Samuel ushered his wife up the walk-way onto the deck where other passengers were waiting. 'Trust in the Lord, my dear.'

Jean nodded firmly. That was after all the only thing to do.

After the nerve-wracking journey and some sea-sickness no doubt the Rutherfords arrived in London. When Samuel and the other Scottish delegates arrived at the Assembly, they were given a great welcome. Their advice and expertise would be of great help over the next four years.

It was quite an honour to be asked to represent the Church of Scotland at such a gathering, thought Samuel. But even in the midst of all the excitement and honour, he still looked back with longing to the quieter days of Anwoth, the rolling hills, the songbirds and Rutherford's Walk. However, Samuel could see the importance of this meeting he had been called to. What was decided at these discussions would likely be the foundation of many good things in the future.

One of these good things was called *The Westminster Shorter Catechism*. A document that is still widely published today. Because Samuel knew quite a bit about catechisms he was very influential in the writing of this one. Samuel had, after all, spent a lot of time in Anwoth writing a catechism of his own which he had used with the young people in his congregation.

The Shorter Catechism was called that because it was shorter than *The Larger Catechism* and it was also a collection of questions and answers that were simpler and therefore easier to memorise. What a project to be involved in! What an assembly to be part of! Though Samuel must have felt homesick at times, he was thrilled to be doing the Lord's work for the Lord's people.

It was wonderful to see the greatest theological minds from both sides of the border working together. Another cross-border project that took place around this time was a united effort by both nations and their churches to resist the tyrant Charles I. This was a treaty called 'The Solemn League and Covenant.'[2] Its aim was to reform Christianity across England and Ireland, to emulate that which had already taken place in Scotland. The English Puritans were now fighting for political freedoms as well as religious ones and they wanted to know if Scotland would be on their side. The treaty was firstly a commitment to preserve the reformed religion in the Church of Scotland and reform religion in England and Ireland so that the church in those lands was in keeping with the Word of God. Secondly, Roman Catholic practices were to be exterminated. Thirdly, Parliament and the rights of the two kingdoms of Scotland and England were to be protected. In addition to this they also agreed to protect the king's person and authority. It wasn't a document that threatened the king's life in any way. Those who signed the Covenant also promised to lead a holy life.

---

2. The Solemn League and Covenant was signed prior to the Scots participation at the Westminster Assembly. It is in the light of this treaty that the Westminster Assembly took place.

The Law, the Prince and the Scribe

It was important that those who followed the Reformed faith stood together in this way. For if you looked across the channel to other countries you could see the powers of the Pope and Roman Catholic authorities plotting to thwart the Reformation. Not that far away in Ireland there had been a massacre of 40,000 Protestants. And the Covenanters knew that there were men of power in England who supported actions like these. The Covenanters, the Puritans and other godly men had to unite to present a single front.

And in most things it seemed that the Covenanters and the Puritans were in agreement – even when they disagreed they did so in a way that showed Christian patience and love. Some of the men at the Westminster Assembly really enjoyed the cut and thrust of debate, and they all recognised the importance of what they were doing. In the end all the points they made had to be supported by the Word of God.

The biggest disagreement that the delegates had was what was the best form of Church government – some still wanted Episcopacy, others like Samuel Rutherford felt that Presbyterianism was the only choice, there were still others who thought that everyone should be Independent. In fact, quite a lot of the men in the English Parliament were Independents and they were led by a man called Oliver Cromwell. Samuel began to wonder if this independence movement could be even more dangerous than Episcopacy. 'If every congregation is allowed to do what it likes then we are laying ourselves open to chaos. But even though I disagree with these men,' Samuel deliberated, 'I know they are all gracious. They may differ from me in what I think but I see that they walk with God.'

However, once more into the debate strode the monarch! In the middle of it all Charles I started to cause problems – again! He declared that any man involved with the Westminster Assembly was a rebel. Nobody took any notice of him and the assembly carried on.

As well as the catechism the assembly delegates were working on a document called *The Westminster Confession of Faith*. This document explained the doctrines[3] behind Reformed theology.[4]

Points that Samuel and others had discovered through a lifetime of reading God's Word and living by it, were written in detail in this book so that it was clear what the Reformers stood for. One of the central points was that God is sovereign in all things and it is He who chooses or elects individuals to receive salvation.

The Confession of Faith was a summary of the foundations of the reformed faith. At times like this it was a relief for Christians to see that God's truth was unchanging, as the nation of England had now fallen into a bloody civil war.

---

3. Doctrines: a set of beliefs.
4. Both the Shorter and Larger Catechism were based on the completed Confession of Faith.

The Law, the Prince and the Scribe

It was during these years that Samuel wrote that influential book, *Lex Rex*. Samuel penned this political work to counteract King James VI and others like him who said it was treason to disagree with what the king did. *'The power of creating a man a king is from the people,'* Samuel wrote. *'If the king does not have the consent of the people then he is a usurper.'* The king was born into power, but it was a birthright that was borrowed from his people. When a king abused this power they could take it back. That was what Samuel argued, a humble scribe who had the courage to take on a monarchy and a powerful one at that.

Samuel's statements had to be said at this time in history, but again it was a difficult and dangerous period to be expressing yourself in this way. The Marquis of Montrose in Scotland despised Samuel for publishing this book. Charles I of course was infuriated.

Samuel must have longed to be in his own country rather than staying as a guest of a nation that was fighting amongst itself. Oliver Cromwell and the Parliamentarians also called Roundheads were now fighting against the Royalists who were known as Cavaliers. It was hard enough to be in a strange land, but at such a time as this. Samuel would have preferred to be back in Scotland. At least he had, in London, the occasional opportunity to preach. Once or twice he was even allowed to preach a sermon to the English Parliament.

Sadly, both he and Jean had a hard time in London. More of their children died. It seems that trouble and grief were never far away from the life of Samuel Rutherford. However, as always, he could in his correspondence offer heart-felt sympathy to others who suffered the same pain. When he heard good news and bad from north of the border he would pick up his pen once again to give words of advice and encouragement and when his friend Marion M'Naught passed away, words of comfort to her family.

In thinking about death, Samuel Rutherford would often write passionate poetic portions that would be a comfort to himself and others as they faced their own final journey or the passing away of those close to them: *'Our fair morning is at hand; the day-star is near the rising, and we are not many miles from home. What does it matter then if our lives be ill in the smoky rooms of this world! We are not to stay here, and we shall be dearly welcome to Him to whom we are going. Travelling to heaven is a well spent journey though seven deaths lie between. Oh how sweet to be wholly Christ's, and to be wholly in Christ; to dwell in Immanuel's[5] high and blessed land, and live in the sweetest air where no wind blows but the breath of the Holy Spirit, no sea nor floods flow but the pure water of life that floweth from the throne and from the Lamb. Oh when shall the night be gone and the shadows flee away?'*

In writing to a friend about the deaths of two of his children, he pictured the sun-kissed garden at Anwoth where the birds had sung and the roses bloomed, *'Christ the good gardener may pluck His roses and gather His lilies at*

---

5. Immanuel: A name for God or Jesus that means God is with us.

midsummer. What is that to you or me? We should prize Christ above all others. Nothing should be better to us.'

Samuel did finally return to Scotland but not before the Westminster Assembly heaped praises on him. They sent a letter of recommendation to the Church of Scotland. 'We restore him to you with ample testimony of his learning, godliness, faithfulness and diligence and we humbly pray that God our Father will increase the number of such burning and shining lights among you.'

The year 1647 saw Samuel and Jean make the return journey to St. Andrews, this time with no infant in tow. That must have left a bitter taste to the sweet home-coming.

1649 and All That

Samuel may now have lived some distance from the English Civil War, but it didn't mean that Scotland wasn't involved. And even though Cromwell and others like him had supported the Covenanters, this didn't last.

Oliver Cromwell, who was an ardent Independent kicked out several Presbyterians from Parliament. Charles I, who knew his days were numbered if he stayed in England in 1648, had decided to flee to the land of his forebears – and returned to Scotland. Isn't it ironic to see the once 'all powerful' monarch seeking refuge in a land that he had treated so abominably? Then begins another confusing time of history where you're never very sure who is on what side and for how long. The Scottish Parliament agreed to give Charles military support on the condition that he promised to protect the liberty of the Church of Scotland. Charles made that promise, but he had done this sort of thing before. Nobody should trust a liar. Samuel and other Covenanters certainly didn't trust him and said as much.

The Law, the Prince and the Scribe

Soon the countries of Scotland and England were at war. Scotland invaded England only to be crushed by Cromwell and his troops. When the Scottish troops were vanquished, the balance of power shifted again in Scotland and Charles I was delivered back as a captive to the English on the condition that he would not be killed.

However, that year 1649 was the year that Charles I was executed[1] and England was declared a republic – that is a name for a country that is ruled by a parliament and without any king or queen.

The people who had delivered the king into the hands of the English Parliament were stunned and upset when they heard the news, Samuel in particular. Yes, he had written a book against tyrants, but he had warned people specifically in that book against taking the life of the monarch. You could resist a king, that was only defending yourself, and lawful, but killing a king was offensive and unlawful.

The decision of the English Parliament to send Charles I to the executioner's block was not just one bloody incident in history, it was the beginning of yet another even more turbulent period where many men and women were martyred for their faith. Charles I, you see, had a son, a prince who would become Charles II. The Republic of England didn't last that long in the scheme of things and soon Charles II was restored to his father's throne. It only took eleven years.

---

[1]. Charles I was executed on January 30 1649. Oliver Cromwell assumed control of the new English Commonwealth

Samuel Rutherford

Charles II was reinstated to the throne partly through the influence of the Scottish Parliament. They saw him as a Stewart and a Scot. As long as he agreed to the National Covenant and the Solemn League and Covenant they would accept him as king. Charles didn't want to do that, though he didn't mind promising to do it. He'd promise the Scots whatever they wanted so he would get his own way. Then he could easily change his mind. Like father like son as they say!

Samuel Rutherford certainly saw the similarities but could hardly believe that others were so blind. When Charles II came to visit St. Andrews, Samuel was given the opportunity to preach a sermon. Many weaker men would have opted to say something pleasant and uncontroversial – not Samuel. He pointed out that kings and princes were there as servants of the people. And that it was Charles' responsibility to protect the Covenants [2] that his people had made.

Oliver Cromwell heard of the agreement between Charles and the Scots and was soon on his way with an army to engage in battle. This time Samuel was on the defeated side. He wasn't a soldier, but he preached to the Covenanter army to encourage them. However, the Covenanters lost. Time and time again the English troops defeated them.

Eventually Cromwell was in power in Scotland and was soon forcing his opinions and decisions on

---

2. The National Covenant of 1638 and the Solemn League and Covenant of 1643.

The Law, the Prince and the Scribe

the land. Samuel Rutherford didn't support Cromwell but neither did he support Charles II either. What a confusing time to live in. Enemies to your right; Opponents to your left! This led to a very bitter disagreement between Samuel and other Scottish Christians. The Church split down the middle. Nobody could agree anymore. They couldn't even discuss things civilly. Everybody was at each other's throats. Even Rutherford was so angry with people, he unjustly accused them and turned away from being their friend. What a dreadful time for the country and the church.

It seemed that even Rutherford for a time had lost the memory of Christ and His beauty. His sermons seemed to focus on the divisions and disagreements until one day something changed – it was about fifteen minutes before the end of his sermon when he started to list the names and titles of Jesus that were in the Bible. One after another came out from his lips, beautiful terms like 'Wonderful Counsellor. Prince of Peace. The Rose of Sharon. The Bright and Morning Star. The Lord of Glory. The Bread of Life. The Water of Life ...' on and on they came.

Samuel paused for a minute then a nobleman stood up and urged him to stop where he was. 'You have it there,' he declared. Nobody wanted Samuel to return to the old disagreeable ways now that he had started once more to preach about Christ.

In the years ahead, Samuel did much of the same things that he had ever done. As well as preaching and

Samuel Rutherford

letter writing he wrote more books. He and his wife also had three more children. However, in that period two of them died.

Oliver Cromwell also perished, and his son who took on his duties did not do a good job. Eventually the monarchy was restored. Charles II was crowned at Westminster Abbey – he had finally got his way. Did he remember any of the promises he had made? He probably remembered them, but he certainly didn't keep them. He ruled his lands in much the same way as his father had – with an iron fist. The Earl of Argyle who had crowned him in Scotland in 1651 came to London for the coronation at Westminster. He was a leading Covenanter. Charles II had him thrown in the tower of London.

It was just the beginning of another period of persecution that would soon be infamous throughout the land as 'The Killing Times'.

A close friend of Rutherford's called James Guthrie was thrown in prison in Edinburgh. Samuel wrote him a letter. He knew something of what his friend was going through. Although his time in Aberdeen hadn't been behind bars, his freedoms had been removed from him. He knew that his friend was going through a very difficult experience, *'It is the cause of Christ that you now suffer for, but fear not. You are not, you shall not be alone. The Father is with you ... Christ is Captain of the castle and Lord of the keys. The cooling waters that refresh you from the water of God's promises are more than the frownings of the furnace.'*

The Law, the Prince and the Scribe

Samuel could see the way the wind was turning and wondered how long it would take before the icy blast of persecution reached his door. Charles II was out for revenge. Bishops were reinstated in the Church of England and Royalists put into power in the Scottish Parliament. The Covenanters, especially Rutherford were under threat.

Samuel's book *Lex Rex* was banned and burned in Edinburgh and St. Andrews. From the front door of his apartments Samuel could smell the pungent smoke as more and more paper with his words on it was set alight in front of the university. It scratched at his nostrils, and a chill came over his heart. Trouble was coming, of that he was sure.

One little girl was all the family he and Jean had now – Agnes, just eleven years old. Now he wondered what the future would hold for the little lass in his care, and then there was Jean his ever-helpful, ever-loving wife. He could only leave them and his worries with his Lord Jesus.

Although Samuel could often be down in the dumps, sometimes he would see the good in a bad situation. Samuel decided that the persecution and conflict that was once again rampant across Scotland had brought some advantages. 'The divisions that we once had in the church are dissolving away like snow.' The men who had not that long ago been fighting each other with cruel words and evil looks were now drawing together. Christ was their Captain and under

Samuel Rutherford

His command they became as one. It was something sweet in all the bitter circumstances the nation and the church were facing.

Eventually though, what Samuel had been expecting to happen, happened. He was removed from his position at the University of St. Andrews without any pay. Despite this and even with his health at such a low ebb, Rutherford continued to write letters to men and women across the land: to those pastors who had been removed from their ministries only to have Episcopalians replace them; to those congregations who had those men forced on them; to other faithful believers who grieved to see the nation of Scotland so completely lost.

The letters took longer to write as his hand shook and he grew ever weaker. Samuel could see that the sands of time were sinking and that one day soon he would wake in a different world with a different dawn. Even in sickness, the poet was always thinking, always writing, always dreaming of Immanuel's land.

Then in March 1661 a summons came to Samuel Rutherford charging him with treason and demanding that he make his way to Edinburgh to face these charges immediately. This could have resulted in Rutherford's death and martyrdom, but by God's grace it did not.

When the message arrived Samuel was laid out on his sickbed. The proposed journey to Edinburgh was simply impossible. He respectfully asked a friend to write in reply, *'Tell them that I have got a summons already before a superior judge. I will answer my first summons and before the day is over I will be where few kings or great folks ever come.'*

Jean and Agnes were never far away from his bedside. Rutherford had had nine children in total and Agnes was the only one left alive. He weakly turned to her in his last hours and whispered, *'I have left you upon the Lord.'*

On the afternoon of the day before his death it was as though he knew without a doubt that his last hours had arrived, *'This night I will close the door and fasten my anchor within the veil and I shall go away in a sleep by five in the morning.'*

This was exactly what happened.

On 29 March, 1661 Samuel Rutherford died, his last words were, *'Glory, glory dwelleth in Immanuel's land.'*

Samuel Rutherford was mourned by all the godly in the land and buried in the churchyard of the Chapel of Saint Regulus, St. Andrews.

Samuel Rutherford's Grave

Samuel Rutherford's gravestone can be found today at the Old Cathedral graveyard in St. Andrews at the foot of the ruined wall. On the gravestone the epitaph describes his passion for Jesus Christ:

> What tongue, what pen, or skill of men
> Can famous Rutherford commend!
> His learning justly rais'd his fame
> True goodness did adorn his name.
> He did converse with things above,
> Acquainted with Immanuel's love.
> Most orthodox he was and sound,
> And many errors did confound.
> For Zion's King, and Zion's cause,
> And Scotland's covenanted laws,
> Most constantly he did contend,
> Until his time was at an end.
> At last he won to full fruition
> Of that which he had seen in vision.

Samuel Rutherford Timeline

1600	Samuel Rutherford birth.
1603	Queen Elizabeth 1 dies. James VI and I (son of Mary Queen of Scots) was Elizabeth's successor. The nations of Scotland and England were then united under one crown. King James was a supporter of the Episcopalian church system – not the Presbyterian one that the Scots largely supported.
1605	Gunpowder Plot.
1606	Pocahontas saves life of John Smith.
1610	King James ruled that bishops were to be in charge of the Scottish church once again. Galileo sees the moons of Jupiter through his telescope.
1616	William Shakespeare dies.
1618	Five Articles of Perth. A year after Samuel began his studies at the university of Edinburgh something called the Five Articles of Perth was brought into effect – an attempt by King James to impose the practices of the Episcopalian Church of England on the Church of Scotland.
1620	Pilgrim Fathers arrive at Plymouth on the Mayflower.
1623	Rutherford was appointed as Professor of Humanities at Edinburgh University.

1625	James I died and his son Charles I succeeded him.
1627	Rutherford was installed at Anwoth as minister.
1629	Charles 1 dissolved the English Parliament which resulted in eleven years where he was an absolute monarch with no limits on his power.
1630	Rutherford's wife and children die.
1631	The Taj Mahal is built in India.
1636	Rutherford's book against Arminianism published. Rutherford disposed from his congregation and exiled to Aberdeen.
1637	Scots refuse to accept Laud's liturgy.
1638	National covenant signed. Rutherford leaves Aberdeen. Presbyterianism re-established in Scotland
1639-40	Bishops Wars.
1642-48	First and Second Civil Wars.
1643	Signing of Solemn League and Covenant.
1643-49	Westminster Assembly, Confession of Faith, Shorter Catechism.
1644	Lex Rex Published.
1649	Charles I executed.
1651	Charles II crowned at Scone in Scotland.
1660	Charles II restored to the monarchy.
1661	Samuel Rutherford dies.

Bibliography

31 Days with Samuel Rutherford, Rev J Lewis, Lewis Publishing, 2013.

Samuel Rutherford; Scots Worthies series; Neil M Ross, Scottish Reformation Society, Edinburgh, 2018.

A History of the Scottish People, 1560-1830, T C Smout, Fontana Press, 1998.

Letters of Samuel Rutherford, Rev Andrew Bonar, Portage Publications, Colorado Springs, 2006.

Origins of the Declaration of Independence: Samuel Rutherford's 'Lex, Rex' by David Kopel Contributor, The Volokh Conspiracy. https://www.washingtonpost.com/news/volokh-conspiracy/wp/2016/07/02/origins-of-the-declaration-of-independence-samuel-rutherfords-lex-rex/?noredirect=on&utm_term=.81fba1beb02d.

Politics Religion and the British Revolutions – John Coffey, Cambridge University Press, Cambridge, 2010.

Samuel Rutherford; (Bitesize Biographies) – Richard M Hannula, EP Books, Darlington, 2016.

Samuel Rutherford and his Friends, Faith Cook, Banner of Truth, Edinburgh, 2013.

Samuel Rutherford, Rev Andrew Thomson, Hodder and Stoughton, London, 1884.

Samuel Rutherford, A New biography of the Man and his ministry, Kingsley Rendell, Christian Focus Publications, Fearn, 2003.

The Life of Samuel Rutherford, Thomas Murray, William Oliphant, Glasgow, 1728.

Fact File: Anne Cousin
1824-1906

Many who don't know Samuel Rutherford know a hymn which they often think was written by him called 'Immanuel's Land' or 'The Sands of Time are Sinking.' This hymn was in fact written by Anne Cousin who was the widow of the Rev. William Cousin, late Minister of the Free Church of Melrose. It was first published in *The Christian Treasury* 1857. 'The Sands of Time are Sinking' is a hymn based largely on the words of Samuel Rutherford. The whole hymn or poem lasts for nineteen verses – here are some of the most familiar ones.

The Sands of Time are Sinking

The sands of time are sinking,
The dawn of Heaven breaks;
The summer morn I've sighed for—
The fair, sweet morn awakes:
Dark, dark hath been the midnight,
But dayspring is at hand,
And glory, glory dwelleth
In Immanuel's land.

O Christ, He is the fountain,
The deep, sweet well of love!
The streams on earth I've tasted
More deep I'll drink above:
There to an ocean fullness
His mercy doth expand,
And glory, glory dwelleth
In Immanuel's land.

The King there in His beauty,
Without a veil is seen:
It were a well spent journey,
Though seven deaths lay between:
The Lamb with His fair army,
Doth on Mount Zion stand,
And glory—glory dwelleth
In Immanuel's land.

The little birds of Anwoth,
I used to count them blessed,
Now, beside happier altars
I go to build my nest:
O'er these there broods no silence,

No graves around them stand,
For glory, deathless, dwelleth
　　In Immanuel's land.

Fair Anwoth by the Solway,
To me thou still art dear,
E'en from the verge of Heaven,
I drop for thee a tear.
Oh! If one soul from Anwoth
Meet me at God's right hand,
My heav'n will be two heavens,
　　In Immanuel's land.
I've wrestled on towards Heaven,

Against storm and wind and tide,
Now, like a weary traveller
That leaneth on his guide,
Amid the shades of evening,
While sinks life's lingering sand,
I hail the glory dawning
From Immanuel's land.
Deep waters crossed life's pathway,

The hedge of thorns was sharp;
Now, these lie all behind me,
Oh! for a well tuned harp!
Oh! To join hallelujah
With yon triumphant band,
Who sing where glory dwelleth
　　In Immanuel's land.
With mercy and with judgment

My web of time He wove,
And aye, the dews of sorrow
Were lustered with His love;

I'll bless the hand that guided,
I'll bless the heart that planned
When throned where glory dwelleth
In Immanuel's land.
I shall sleep sound in Jesus,

Filled with His likeness rise,
To love and to adore Him,
To see Him with these eyes:
'Tween me and resurrection
But paradise doth stand;
Then—then for glory dwelling
In Immanuel's land.
The bride eyes not her garment,

But her dear bridegroom's face;
I will not gaze at glory
But on my king of grace.
Not at the crown He giveth
But on His piercèd hand;
The Lamb is all the glory
Of Immanuel's land.
They've summoned me before them,

But there I may not come,
My Lord says Come up hither,
My Lord says Welcome home!
My king, at His white throne,
My presence doth command
Where glory—glory dwelleth
In Immanuel's land.

Take Away Points

- What you will have learned from reading about the life of Samuel Rutherford.
- God is sovereign and in control. He is the all powerful and mighty God, above all rulers, powers and authorities.
- As God's creation and human beings we have duties and we have rights.
- We can and will suffer in life but this is all part of God's plan.
- Sin is a danger to our bodies and our souls.
- God's Word is a blessing.
- Jesus Christ is lovely.
- Do not be afraid to stand up for Christ, His church and God's Word.
- There is another world, the Kingdom of God or heaven, where one day the believer will be at rest, without sin and in great joy.

Thinking Further Topics

After each chapter you can read the thinking further topic for that chapter so that you can discuss the life of Samuel Rutherford with friends and family, maybe as part of a book group. Or you can just think about his life and your life and about what God wants you to learn from the life of this particular Christian man.

A Wild and Windswept Scribe

Bible Reference: Deuteronomy 13:4, Revelation 3:3
Have you ever had to leave your home to go and live somewhere new? How did you feel? Perhaps you felt like Samuel – nervous and excited. Our emotions can be difficult and confusing sometimes. Particularly when life throws us a challenge. Samuel's prayer at the end of the night uses words that he wrote down some years later. 'May I fasten my hold firmly upon Christ. How do you make sure you have a firm hold on Christ?

Firstly you need to believe that Christ has a firm hold on you. The Bible tells us that Jesus will never let us out of His grasp. No one will ever snatch you out of His hand once you have trusted in Jesus (John 10:28). Then you must keep your eyes on Jesus by reading God's Word and asking God for His help in understanding and obeying what you read.

Songbirds by the Solway

Bible Reference: Romans 2:13

Do you ever decide to put something off for another day? Perhaps you have a job to do but you say to yourself, 'I'll get around to it. I'll do it tomorrow.' Samuel believed that it would have been better if he'd decided to trust in God sooner than he did. And it is always right not to disobey God or to delay in obeying Him. Samuel delayed in becoming a Christian.

Now it is God who saves us from sin and is in control of all our life. We do, however, have a duty to obey Him and respond to God's call to believe in Him. We must say yes to God. We have no excuse to say, 'No, I'll do it tomorrow.' We can't be sure if we will have a tomorrow. The Bible says 'Now is the accepted time. Now is the day of salvation.' (2 Corinthians 6:2). You must trust in Jesus now.

Always Writing, Always Preaching

Bible Reference: Col 3:12, James 5:7

When do you feel most impatient? Is it when you are waiting for a special day to arrive? Perhaps it is when you are hungry and there is still a whole hour to wait before dinner? Patience is often described as a virtue – a good trait or characteristic. Sometimes with some effort we can show patience but Jesus shows great patience with us. We don't deserve to be treated as well as God treats us. We can be impatient with God, but God knows our weaknesses and loves to show mercy. When we next get impatient with others, or perhaps even with God, we should relax and realise that God is in control. Remember though that we should never test God's patience. God can patiently wait for you to obey Him, but He will not always be patient. There will come a day when God's patience with sinners will end. You only have this life to repent and turn to God.

Set Your Arrow Straight

Bible Reference: John 3:16-17

Think about what Christ went through on the cross and why He did it. This was often the theme of Samuel Rutherford's sermons. Christ's love bound Him to the cross. He suffered physical pain and death, emotional and spiritual pain because He was abandoned by His friends. Even God, the Father, turned His back on Him. This was all God's plan for salvation – that Christ, His Son should suffer in this way instead of sinners. Christ's suffering has freed you from the guilt of sin. If you trust in Him you are forgiven and saved. Eternal life is yours.

Letters, a Disguise and Tragedy

Bible Reference: Psalm 133:1

The story of Archbishop Usher is quite amusing, isn't it? But although it is funny it also teaches us some important points.

- Don't judge a book by its cover. What you see is not always what you get. Appearances can be deceptive. Usher looked like a tramp, so although he was shown hospitality the maid and even Mrs Rutherford assumed Archbishop Usher was one.
- It is important to be in unity with other Christians. We may not agree on everything but when we trust in the same Saviour and believe and follow God's Word that is a blessing. Sometimes when we disagree, we have to push back especially if God's Word is under attack. But when there are disagreements that are not worth fighting about, we should ask God to help us show love and be friends when this would give most glory to Him.

Real Friends and Real Enemies

Bible Reference: Isaiah 41:10, Psalm 3:6

Not being allowed to preach was painful to Samuel. It was what God had called him to do. Sometimes due to sickness or other troubles we can no longer do the things we once enjoyed. Samuel, however, realised eventually that his suffering in Aberdeen had been good for him. In his suffering he learned new things about Christ. When we read God's Word, we should look out for His promises. Did you know that in the Bible it says 'Fear not' at least 366 times – once for every day of the year and a leap year.

Events Belong to God

Bible Reference: John 14:6

Samuel told some stories about ships at sea. You may not have been on a ship that has a deck, a steering wheel or a compass. But you probably have driven in a car or perhaps you've flown in a plane? A car needs a driver to turn the steering wheel. A plane requires a captain to plot the route and navigate towards a safe landing. Our lives are like a ship, a car and a plane. They need to be steered – but they need to be steered by Jesus. You need Him to direct you through the Word of God. You must be willing to let God be in charge. Don't sit there thinking that it doesn't matter what you believe. The pilot never says it doesn't matter what I do or where I go. He knows he has to be precise about his landing. Remember that getting to heaven is just if not more precise. You can only get eternal life through Jesus Christ our Lord. Jesus says 'I am the way, the truth and the life. No one comes to the father except through me.'

The King who Huffed and Puffed

Bible Reference: Genesis 4:7

Samuel's challenge to the young men he taught was an important one. It is something that young men and young women should learn from. The choices you make when you are young can have a huge impact on your future life. When you are young let God take charge of your decisions. Be guided by Him. If you don't, Satan will help himself to the best part of your life, strength and passions.

Think about what you most like to do. What do you do first thing when you wake up? What do you do last thing at night before you go to sleep? These are both indications of what is most important in your life. You know if someone is healthy if they have a good appetite and are eating healthy food. What about your spiritual appetite? Do you long to spend time with God and His Word? That is an indication of whether you are healthy in your soul.

Look at Scotland!

Bible Reference: Isaiah 7:14, Matt 1:23

Have you ever wanted to be somewhere else? Why do you suppose when people are upset because they are far away it is called homesickness? Is it like a disease? It sounds as though Samuel Rutherford might have been homesick for heaven. Why do you think that heaven is like home to a Christian? The name Immanuel that Samuel used in one of his writings is a name for God or Jesus. It means God with us. Think about what it is like to have God with us. Think about what heaven is going to be like when we have God with us all the time and there will be no sin. How lovely it will be to have Jesus there and to have no sin to destroy our joy.

1649 and All That

Bible References: 1 Tim 2:2, Hebrews 2:3, Rev 7:10

When Samuel received the summons from the court he said in reply he had received another summons to another court – heaven. Samuel knew that he was not long for this world and soon to die. He said he had an appointment in a place where few kings and great people ever came. It is important to note that he said few. Kings can be saved and we should pray for those who rule and reign over us.

Samuel's last words were 'Glory, glory dwelleth in Immanuel's land.' What do you think will be the most glorious thing about heaven? What do you most look forward to? Be sure though to first of all trust in Jesus and ask for your sins to be forgiven. Salvation belongs to Christ. Only those who come to Christ will be saved and given eternal life.

Samuel Rutherford, Democracy and the U.S.A.

Samuel Rutherford in 1644 wrote the book "Lex, Rex, or the Law and the Prince." The main thrust of this book was that the monarch must obey the law, the law being the Law of God. Rutherford stated that The Law is the supreme ruler and not those individuals who rule, be that on the throne or through government. The true source of law is not the king's will, but God's will. Laws made by kings that are not consistent with the law of God are not true law.

Rutherford proclaimed that the foundation of law and government should be The Word of God rather than the opinions of men. All men, including the king were under the law of God.

Lex Rex is widely recognised as one of the most valuable defences of democratic government ever written. Much of it has influenced the foundations and wording of constitutions around the world.

Rutherford believed in the right of self-defence. He believed that the people had a right to bear arms and armour in order to defend themselves: 'To denude the people of armour because they may abuse the prince, is to expose them to violence and oppression, unjustly.' Rutherford also argued that, 'armour, forts, and strongholds' although they belonged to the king in name were actually the possession of the people.

It's important to note that Samuel Rutherford was no rampant revolutionary. He only believed that a revolution was necessary if the monarch was bent on destroying society and its people.

The American Declaration of Independence stated that a government should not be changed on a whim but only when there had been 'a long train of abuses'. Then and only then 'it is the people's right, it is their duty, to throw off such Government'.

Samuel Rutherford maintained that the people had three options to turn to when dealing with corrupt rulers: Supplication, Flight and then Force as the last resort.

You can see Rutherford's influence again in the Declaration of Independence when the Americans stated that their protests had been constantly rejected. As they did not have the option to flee conflict was their only reasonable choice.

Rutherford also stated that 'it is lawful to repel violence by violence.' Sometimes he said that tyrants were a judgment sent by God because of the sins of the people. But that it was still within the rights of the people to resist that tyrant. God can send a famine on a guilty nation, but it is still lawful for that nation to attempt to grow crops to feed itself.

The Law, the Prince and the Scribe

Samuel's world view has had a profound influence on the thoughts and lives of your world and mine. If you live in a western democracy the foundations of that democracy owe much to what Samuel Rutherford thought and wrote.

Samuel believed in the Word of God and its inerrancy and this influenced every area of his life including his politics. His politics, through Lex Rex, influenced colonial America through two gentlemen: John Locke and John Witherspoon. John Witherspoon was a Presbyterian minister educated at Edinburgh University and then professor at Princeton University. He brought the principles of Samuel Rutherford and Lex Rex across the Atlantic. He was the only clergyman to sign the Declaration of Independence and a member of Congress from 1776 to 1779 and from 1780 to 1782. Witherspoon influenced America through his impact on his students many of whom held positions of power in the early years of American history.

Map of the British Isles in Samuel Rutherford's Time

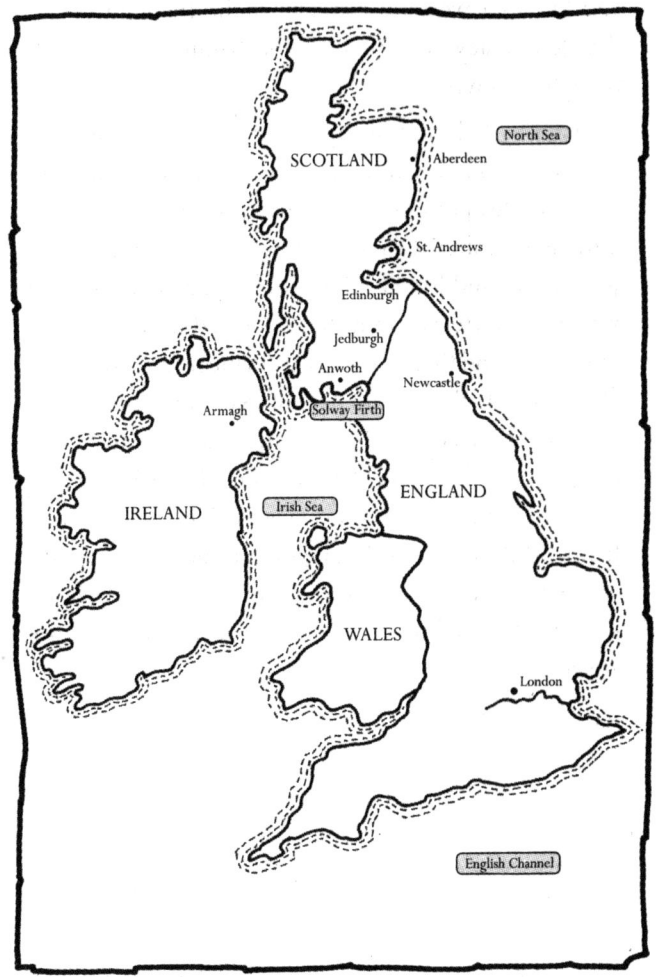

The Westminster Assembly of 1643 to 1649 produced three documents of lasting value to the Church: The Westminster Confession of Faith, The Larger Catechism, and The Shorter Catechism. Since then, The Shorter Catechism has become well known as a manual of doctrine for both children and adults who require an introduction to the Christian faith. It is an ideal way to give structure to the discipling of new believers. This edition contains the addition of Scripture proof texts and notes by Roderick Lawson.

ISBN: 978-1-78191-810-4

Using familiar puzzle formats such as word searches, crossword puzzles and codes this book will help children to work through the Westminster Shorter Catechism – one of the church's statements of faith. The Shorter Catechism covers the following important doctrines: God; Sin; Christ; The ten commandments; Baptism; The Lord's Supper and The Lord's prayer.

ISBN: 978-1-84550-722-0

This is the true story of one of Scotland's most adventurous preachers. As the son-in-law of another fiery Scot – John Knox – John Welch was bound to cause a stir – and he did! Find out about how he conquered ruffians, saved a town from the dreaded plague and even dodged a cannon ball!

Extra Features include: Maps, Quiz, Time Line, What was life like then? and Fact Summaries.

ISBN: 978-1-78191-604-9

OTHER BOOKS IN THE TRAIL BLAZERS SERIES

Augustine, The Truth Seeker
ISBN 978-1-78191-296-6

John Calvin, After Darkness Light
ISBN 978-1-78191-550-9

Fanny Crosby, The Blind Girl's Song
ISBN 978-1-78191-163-1

John Chrysostom, The Preacher in the Emperor's Court
ISBN: 978-1-5271-0308-5

Elisabeth Elliot, Do the Next Thing
ISBN: 978-1-5271-0161-6

John Knox, The Sharpened Sword
ISBN 978-1-78191-057-3

Eric Liddell, Finish the Race
ISBN 978-1-84550-590-5

Martin Luther, Reformation Fire
ISBN 978-1-78191-521-9

Robert Moffat, Africa's Brave Heart
ISBN 978-1-84550-715-2

D.L. Moody, One Devoted Man
ISBN 978-1-78191-676-6

Mary of Orange, At the Mercy of Kings
ISBN 978-1-84550-818-0

Patrick of Ireland: The Boy who Forgave
ISBN: 978-1-78191-677-3

Elizabeth Prentiss, More Love
ISBN: 978-1-5271-0299-6

Francis & Edith Schaeffer, Taking on the World
ISBN: 978-1-5271-0300-9

John Stott, The Humble Leader
ISBN 978-1-84550-787-9

Ulrich Zwingli, Shepherd Warrior
ISBN 978-1-78191-803-6

* * *

For a full list of Trail Blazers, please see our website: www.christianfocus.com

Look out for the Trail Blazer box sets:

Arts and Science: 978-1-78191-639-1
Heroes and Heroines: 978-1-78191-638-4
Reformers and Activists: 978-1-78191-637-7
Preachers and Teachers: 978-1-78191-636-0
Missionaries and Medics: 978-1-78191-635-3
Evangelists and Pioneers: 978-1-78191-634-6

All Trail Blazers are available as e-books.

Christian Focus Publications publishes books for adults and children under its four main imprints: Christian Focus, CF4K, Mentor and Christian Heritage. Our books reflect our conviction that God's Word is reliable and Jesus is the way to know him, and live for ever with him.

Our children's publication list includes a Sunday School curriculum that covers pre-school to early teens, and puzzle and activity books. We also publish personal and family devotional titles, biographies and inspirational stories that children will love.

If you are looking for quality Bible teaching for children then we have an excellent range of Bible stories and age-specific theological books.

From pre-school board books to teenage apologetics, we have it covered!

Find us at our web page:
www.christianfocus.com